BEYOND INDIVIDUALISM

*Religion, Culture, and Public Life*

## Religion, Culture, and Public Life

SERIES EDITOR: KAREN BARKEY

The resurgence of religion calls for careful analysis and constructive criticism of new forms of intolerance, as well as new approaches to tolerance, respect, mutual understanding, and accommodation. In order to promote serious scholarship and informed debate, the Institute for Religion, Culture, and Public Life and Columbia University Press are sponsoring a book series devoted to the investigation of the role of religion in society and culture today. This series includes works by scholars in religious studies, political science, history, cultural anthropology, economics, social psychology, and other allied fields whose work sustains multidisciplinary and comparative as well as transnational analyses of historical and contemporary issues. The series focuses on issues related to questions of difference, identity, and practice within local, national, and international contexts. Special attention is paid to the ways in which religious traditions encourage conflict, violence, and intolerance and also support human rights, ecumenical values, and mutual understanding. By mediating alternative methodologies and different religious, social, and cultural traditions, books published in this series will open channels of communication that facilitate critical analysis.

For the list of titles in this series, see page 207–8.

# BEYOND INDIVIDUALISM

*The Challenge of Inclusive Communities*

George Rupp

Columbia University Press
New York

Columbia University Press

*Publishers Since 1893*

New York    Chichester, West Sussex

cup.columbia.edu

Copyright © 2015 Columbia University Press

Library of Congress Cataloging-in-Publication Data

Rupp, George.

Beyond individualism : the challenge of inclusive communities / George Rupp.

pages cm. — (Religion, culture, and public life)

Includes bibliographical references and index.

ISBN 978-0-231-17428-2 (cloth : alk. paper)—ISBN 978-0-231-53986-9 (e-book)

1. Communitarianism. 2. Individualism. 3. Religious communities. I. Title.

HM758.R87 2015

302.5'4—dc23                                                        2015000383

Columbia University Press books are printed on permanent and durable acid-free paper.

This book is printed on paper with recycled content.

Printed in the United States of America

c 10 9 8 7 6 5 4 3 2 1

Cover & interior design: Martin N. Hinze.

References to websites (URLs) were accurate at the time of writing. Neither the author nor Columbia University Press is responsible for URLs that may have expired or changed since the manuscript was prepared.

For Nancy—
my closest companion for fifty-five years

# Contents

# Acknowledgments

MY ACKNOWLEDGMENTS could be either endlessly extensive or blessedly brief. It is a tough choice. But I select the short version.

As readers will note quite quickly, for the writing of this book I am enormously indebted to collaborators in multiple institutions. While I certainly include among those institutions Columbia University, Rice University, and Harvard University, in the front ranks are my colleagues in the International Rescue Committee. In that cohort are staff at IRC headquarters in New York City and also board members and donors. But I think especially of coworkers across the United States and around the world who are the foundation of IRC programs and who again and again welcomed me generously and provided indispensable elucidation of the issues I discuss in this book. I am deeply grateful to each of them individually and to all of them together.

I am also thankful to those who contributed very directly to my writing of the book itself: Vartan Gregorian and the Carnegie Corporation of New York for the grant that supported my year as a Senior Fellow at the Carnegie Council for Religion in International Affairs; and Joel Rosenthal along with our Carnegie Council for Ethics in International Affairs colleagues for engagement with the project, which included participation in Carnegie Council centennial celebrations in Edinburgh, Sarajevo, and New York.

For even more direct help in preparing the constituent parts of the book, I thank Brenda Berg-Morrow, my indispensable colleague at the International Rescue Committee, and Andreas Rekdal, who provided very effective support at the Carnegie Council in processing the final manuscript.

I am grateful as well to all who contributed more directly to the publication itself: to Karen Barkey, the editor of the series for the Institute for

Religion, Culture, and Public Life in which the book appears, who was very generous in her advice and support; to the anonymous reviewers who expressed appreciation and also offered helpful advice for revisions; and to Columbia University Press staff who oversaw the publishing process—Wendy Lochner, Christine Dunbar, Kathryn Jorge, and their colleagues.

Finally, I express heartfelt appreciation and affection to my partner Nancy, to whom this book is dedicated.

# BEYOND INDIVIDUALISM

# Introduction

AT THE OUTSET, I forewarn readers that the initial pages of this introduction will be more self-referential than is my usual practice or my preference. I am responding to the recommendation of one of the reviewers of the manuscript for this book and also of Karen Barkey, the editor of this series, that I offer some initial autobiographical reflections to set the context for the wide-ranging essays that follow. I am therefore providing an overview of the personal and professional engagements that underlie the themes I develop in the later substantive chapters—along with the invitation to any and all readers who are impatient with such self-indulgence to proceed directly to the final five paragraphs of the introduction.

As I reflect on the more than five decades of my adult life, I am struck by how much my concerns and preoccupations have persisted through the years. The themes of commitment and community constitute an enduring substratum, even if they are expressed in quite different ways. In some respects, these fifty years are framed by or bookended with remarkably similar crosscurrents. In the 1960s, the challenge was to turn ideals into action, which I experienced intensely through my participation in the civil rights movement from the early years of the decade and my opposition to the war in Vietnam from 1964 on. So, too, current events cry out for practical realization of long-voiced aspirations that confront ever more deeply entrenched interests and institutional patterns.

One lesson of the intervening decades is that moving from ideals to new realities is a painstakingly slow process subject to remarkably persistent opposition and frustratingly effective countermeasures. I remember vividly how some of my closest friends in the anti-Vietnam War movement were incredulous when my wife and I decided to live in Ceylon (now

Sri Lanka) for a year with our then one-year-old daughter Kathy, during which Nancy would finish her master's thesis on George Eliot and I would study Theravāda Buddhism. The year was 1969. I had already been deeply involved in anti-Vietnam War efforts since 1964, when I had become an early member of Americans for Reappraisal of Far Eastern Policy (ARFEP). It seemed to me then that the need for a fundamental change in our nation's involvement in Vietnam was so inescapable that it would necessarily take place soon, but some of my cohorts disagreed sharply—and were proved right when the United States remained deeply engaged in the war effort until 1975.

Efforts to establish and institutionalize civil rights and to overcome the persistent poverty that is in part a result of racial discrimination demonstrate even more dramatically the slow pace and unsteady course of moving from ideals to actual change in long-established social patterns. This tendency in the United States becomes only the more powerful, and at least initially intractable, when the issues are construed globally. Yet, domestically and internationally, small steps in positive directions are discernible, even as reversals and setbacks are also evident both in fact and as an ever-present threat.

Beginning with my early participation in the civil rights and anti-Vietnam War movements, I have had the privilege of traveling and living in refreshingly varied settings both in this country and abroad. My most intense involvement in civil rights activities (which included not only demonstrations but also being arrested and going to jail) was based in a predominantly African American church in Jersey City, where I also became an active member of the Congress of Racial Equality (CORE). Even during the three years that I lived in Princeton as an undergraduate, I attended a predominantly African American church. While I am the son of German immigrants and spoke German before I learned English, I did not travel outside of North America until 1962, when I studied in Munich during my junior year of college. But in the course of that year I got to know my relatives, almost all of them for the first time, and traveled widely in Europe. My family and I—by then Nancy, Kathy, and a second daughter,

Stephanie—lived in Germany again during a sabbatical (the only one I have ever had) in 1976, this time in a village of some one thousand inhabitants in the countryside outside Tübingen.

Growing up as the son of immigrants, becoming involved in African American communities, engaging in at times strident social action for civil rights and against the Vietnam War, living in and traveling throughout Europe and Asia, and studying multiple religious traditions all contributed to my sense that no single perspective is adequate for viewing all of our only partially shared experience.

Even during the decades of my professional life in higher education, I have had the good fortune of membership in a considerable range of academic communities. The first after I completed my studies was Johnston College in the University of Redlands. Johnston College was a self-described experimental college that prided itself—a pride that I emphatically shared—on having written evaluations based on learning contracts instead of grades, individualized graduation agreements rather than generalized requirements, and no faculty ranks, no academic departments, and no tenure system. In my third year, even though I was the youngest member of the faculty, I became the vice chancellor. It was an exhilarating time.

From Johnston College I returned to Harvard University. I had received my Ph.D. in the study of religion from the Graduate School of Arts and Sciences (GSAS) on the recommendation of a committee that comprised equal representation from GSAS and the Divinity School. What initially attracted me to Harvard (instead of remaining at Yale University, where I had studied for a Bachelor of Divinity), in addition to its faculty in theology and the philosophy of religion, was the Center for the Study of World Religions. That center, which supported my study of Theravāda Buddhism in Sri Lanka, offered a bridge both between Christianity and other religious traditions and between the Divinity School and the Graduate School of Arts and Sciences. Because I believed that this bridging was crucial and was not as well established anywhere else in American higher education (except perhaps at the University of Chicago), I decided to accept an offer that certainly was less than unambiguously attractive: a five-year dead-end appointment to fill in for one of my esteemed teachers, Richard R. Niebuhr, while he was on loan from the Divinity School to the Faculty of Arts and Sciences to help launch an undergraduate program in religion. (I am tempted to note that only at Harvard could there be such a convoluted arrangement, but if I did I would be betraying my awareness that many other academic institutions have similar rigidities.)

I enjoyed teaching at the Divinity School, advising an extraordinarily diverse array of interesting students, participating in wide-ranging and sometimes contentious faculty discussions, and even serving as chair of the Department of Theology. I also appreciated the sabbatical that was part of the appointment; it allowed me to return to Germany during the second year of my appointment and complete a book that I had been working on and a second that I wrote that year. But I did not like having a dead-end appointment. The original arrangement was that the senior colleague for whom I was filling in would return after three years and that my five-year appointment would therefore allow me two further years to plan my next steps. Consequently, I began to look for options that I could explore in the fourth year or later.

Among the academic institutions that joined in the effort to reform higher education in the late 1960s was the University of Wisconsin—more specifically, the University of Wisconsin-Green Bay (UWGB). UWGB was designated as the campus to develop experimental multidisciplinary programs in instruction and research, and it was searching for a dean for academic affairs. My name had come to the search committee from both Johnston College colleagues and also from the network of Danforth Graduate Fellows, a multi-year support grant that I had enjoyed first at Yale and then at Harvard. After an extended process of interviews and a visit to the campus, I was increasingly intrigued with this effort at reform. When I was offered the position and when my wife Nancy indicated that the timing worked for her, we accepted—with the expectation that we would remain in Wisconsin at least until our daughters graduated from high school.

We thoroughly enjoyed our time in Green Bay—the university, the neighborhood school for our daughters, the community, the gorgeous natural surroundings. I was fully engaged in the challenge of developing the curriculum and the cross-disciplinary research programs in ways that preserved traditional strengths while instituting new patterns. Our family also relished the Wisconsin ethos—even the winter weather. Our rule of thumb was that our daughters, six and nine years old when we moved there, would walk the half mile to school unless the temperature was lower than 20 degrees below zero Fahrenheit.

Much as we loved Green Bay, we did not, however, stay as long as we had anticipated. I was invited to return to the Harvard Divinity School as dean; the chance to build further on the foundation of theological inquiry and comparative religion that distinguished the school was too attractive to decline. In my time there as dean, we did indeed revise the curriculum to integrate the history of religions more fully into all of the programs in theological education and, with the strong support of President Derek Bok and the Harvard Corporation, generated substantial resources to institutionalize this set of initiatives.

In chapters 2 and 3 I discuss further my experiences at Harvard and then also at Rice University and Columbia University, including the quite significant differences in the history and the current ethos of each of those institutions. At least for American readers, there is no need to highlight the geographical contrasts represented in southern California, northeastern Wisconsin, Cambridge, Houston, and New York City. But that diversity serves only as a background for the range of settings to which my position as president of the International Rescue Committee (IRC) allowed me to see.

In my role as dean of the Harvard Divinity School, I also had the opportunity to visit some unexpected places, including Thailand, Pakistan, and Kenya (with a side trip prompted by our younger daughter Stephanie to climb Mount Kilimanjaro in Tanzania). During our Columbia years, Nancy and I also undertook personal visits to our daughters, both of whom are professional anthropologists, in the settings of their field research: Kathy in Japan and Stephanie in southeastern Cameroon. But overall, my years at Harvard, Rice, and Columbia brought me to centers of high culture and significant financial resources both in the United States and abroad where there were prosperous alumni/ae as well as others who were actual or potential supporters and who could be encouraged to increase that support. In contrast, my work with the International Rescue Committee allowed me to visit many other interesting places around the world, including many of those in the most dire need of international relief and development assistance.

The opportunities to visit (in most cases repeatedly) for more than a decade such crisis areas as Afghanistan, Pakistan, Azerbaijan, Bosnia and Herzegovina, Croatia, Sudan (in what is now South Sudan as well as in what is still Sudan, from Red Sea State in the east to Darfur in the west), Uganda, Ethiopia, the Democratic Republic of Congo (especially South Kivu and Katanga provinces), Rwanda, Burundi, Liberia, Sierra Leone, Cote d'Ivoire, Mali, the Central African Republic, Indonesia, Myanmar, and Haiti have been extremely illuminating and enormously rewarding. It is always a great privilege to arrive, not as a tourist, but as part of an international team of over twelve thousand staff, 98 percent of whom are local residents, all working together with struggling yet resilient populations to address tough and often life-threatening challenges. In this sense my eleven years at the International Rescue Committee fill out the varied, but still in the end provincial, experience of my professional life in higher education.

To give a little more texture to the visits on behalf of the International Rescue Committee, I will comment on travels to three countries as illustrations: Afghanistan, South Sudan, and Liberia. In each case I visited multiple times—six to Afghanistan, five to Sudan, and four to Liberia. I will not refer to all of the visits, but I will note a few that exemplify the range of my experiences.

My first visit to Afghanistan was in 2002, shortly after I joined the IRC. I was with a delegation of IRC board members that included three former United States ambassadors. Consequently, the U.S. embassy in Kabul insisted that our delegation be accompanied by armed security guards. Had I not been very early in my time with the IRC, I would have refused the offer—and invited the former ambassadors not to travel with us to Afghanistan. But as it turned out, we accepted the armed escort of Afghan troops, in trucks in front of and behind our two-vehicle convoy. The result was that I felt less secure than on any of my later visits there when I had our usual security, namely the acceptance and support of the Afghans with whom we worked. I also became acutely aware that a visit with an armed security detail endangered our staff by suggesting that our programs were politically motivated.

In subsequent visits, I enjoyed the protection of traveling with our unarmed Afghan staff. After such visits to our field sites, I would sometimes pay a courtesy call on the U.S. ambassador back in Kabul. An appointment for fifteen minutes would often stretch to more than two hours as my colleagues and I were pressed for details about areas that U.S. civilian personnel (including the ambassador unless he traveled with armed security) were banned from visiting.

Yet concern for security was certainly not altogether misplaced. My saddest trip to Afghanistan was in August 2008 to convey deeply felt sympathy after four of our staff were murdered. During that trip, I had a vivid sense of the commitment of our colleagues, both expatriate and Afghan, who even in their profound sadness were focused on the continuation of our programs—and who were relieved when I provided assurances that we would indeed continue.

In my first year at the IRC I also visited what would become South Sudan. It is a sparsely populated and all the more gorgeous and fertile region with only very limited educational and health resources. My most vivid memory of that trip is a meeting with women who were graduating from a program with certifications as community health workers. The program attracted participants from throughout the region. Each one had to be nominated by her own village—and in almost all cases, the person selected was the most experienced midwife in the area. Now, equipped with further training, the graduates would return to provide much-needed basic health care across a significant spectrum of villages, a development that the IRC continues to support and one I continued to admire in subsequent visits.

One of those further visits was especially memorable because I was a part of a five-person delegation led by then-United Nations secretary general Kofi Annan in 2005. We had important though ultimately unproductive meetings in Khartoum, wrenching and also exhilarating gatherings in Darfur, and then an important meeting in South Sudan with John Garang, at that point the vice president of Sudan and the man presumed to become president if a peace agreement could be finalized between the north and the south. Tragically, Garang died in a helicopter crash in Uganda two weeks after our meeting, an enormous loss of a Southern Sudanese leader with the stature, the experience, and the capacity to hold together a team of tribal rivals all too frequently in conflict, especially the Dinka and the Nuer.

My last visit to South Sudan was just after the conclusion of the referendum in which the country voted overwhelmingly for independence in 2011. There was euphoria everywhere: the people of South Sudan were at last going to be free to build a country of their own! It is therefore all the more dismaying to witness the terrible infighting and devastation that is consuming the new country only a few years into independence—and a graphic demonstration of the need to develop the capacity for inclusive communities.

As for Liberia, I will note only one vivid contrast between two of my four trips, one that also powerfully demonstrates the need to develop the capacity for inclusive communities. The first one, which occurred in 2003 as yet one more president was being pushed out of office (for good reasons), includes the experience of being forced off the road with my IRC colleagues to make way for an armed convoy escorting Charles Taylor to his presidential palace. The contrasting trip was in 2006, just after Ellen Johnson Sirleaf was elected president. My colleagues and I had the pleasure of meeting with her—as I also did on a subsequent trip to Liberia and in New York as well, both at the IRC and at the Council on Foreign Relations, where I chaired a session at which she spoke. But even more memorable than those meetings is the sense of optimism evident everywhere in the months after her election. The challenge—especially for Liberians but for the rest of us as well—is to support the trajectory that President Ellen Johnson Sirleaf represents over against the terrible alternative embodied by Charles Taylor. This challenge has been only the more daunting in the face of the current ebola crisis.

Against the backdrop of this diverse set of experiences across a considerable range of locations both in this country and abroad, *Beyond Individualism* offers a serial overview of my recent efforts to think and act in ways that resist the power of special interests and press toward more inclusive communities. Many of the following chapters draw on my responses to specific invitations. I have revised those responses to remove references that are either unhelpfully time-bound or tied exclusively to a particular audience, but I have not fundamentally changed the theme or altered my overall approach in the individual pieces. I am confident that these chapters echo and reinforce each other. My hope and my expectation are that repeated emphasis on common motifs will serve to strengthen the overall argument I am advancing.

To put that overall argument bluntly, the modern Western individualism so many of us (including me) know and love has led us into a global dead end—or, to mix metaphors for a slightly more positive image, to a wide channel so shallow that it is tough to navigate without running aground. One indicator of this dead-end or at best shallow passage is the still influential, even if less pervasive, blindness of secular individualism to the continuing power of religious communities. This specific indicator in turn represents a more general set of issues that demands attention.

Action is required now because so many trends today run directly counter to every aspiration for inclusive communities. For example, in many settings where ethnic and religious differences had for long periods been accommodated more or less amicably, tensions have flared to the point of unrestrained animosity and shocking violence. There are similarly perverse trends that threaten the viability of the earth as an ecosystem and that also are dramatically increasing the gap between the rich and the poor.

Along with the action required of us now is the need to educate coming generations about values that go beyond the inadequacies of the modern Western individualism we have inherited and more or less successfully institutionalized. In keeping with this obligation to educate coming generations, the first part of this book will close with one longer and three brief examples of exhortations addressed to students. While I have retained some of the references to the specific settings in which those talks were delivered, I have also at points generalized the themes with the intention of engaging students of all ages in locations across the United States and perhaps even worldwide.

This book calls for education and action, in parts 1 and 2 respectively. Both imperatives are crucial. Only if we commit ourselves to learning and working together can we hope for at least limited and partial success in the admittedly elusive quest for inclusive communities.

# 1    Passionate Conviction
and Inclusive Community

THIS CHAPTER OFFERS in summary form the central claim of this book: modern Western individualism must engage with rather than simply reject the myriad ways that societies worldwide embrace core convictions grounded in particular communities. Individualism as it has evolved in the West is powerfully attractive. Yet it unavoidably encounters concerted opposition from the deeply rooted patterns that it disrupts and in effect would overturn.

## Conviction in a Pluralistic World

Convictions matter. At the very least our own convictions—the affirmations, commitments, and practices that are central to our personal and social identity—matter to us. Yet because we live in an era of unprecedented global interaction, the convictions of people everywhere also matter to all of us whether we know it or not.

We all read about people—and probably know at least a few personally—who are passionately convinced that their convictions are absolutely right and all others are unquestionably wrong. We also have friends, neigh-

---

This chapter draws on a talk given in response to the invitation to deliver the Jack and Lewis Rudin Lecture at Auburn Theological Seminary in New York on May 2, 2004. It incorporates some paragraphs of my Leonard Hastings Schoff Memorial Lectures at Columbia University, delivered in 2003 and later published as *Globalization Challenged: Conviction, Conflict, Community* (New York: Columbia University Press, 2006). I have adapted the lecture for several occasions since then, most recently for a sixtieth anniversary address at International Christian University in Tokyo in September 2013 and a talk at the American Academy in Berlin in May 2014.

bors, and colleagues who decline to debate such convictions and instead call for a stance of unqualified tolerance toward them all. But in an age of globalization, neither of these positions is viable, even if both may have been serviceable in more provincial times.

The standoff between these two positions is illustrated in our everyday experience and etched into our awareness through the media. We see fervent convictions in the headlines. The perpetrators of the horrific tragedy of 9/11 and their imitators since then are extreme examples even among extremists. But there is an ample supply of others. For examples across a range of traditions, think of recent conflicts in Northern Ireland, Chechnya, and Sri Lanka. In the face of all this awful carnage, we cannot but sympathize with the call of Western secular liberalism: religious and other ideological views should be tolerated but must remain private convictions that do not shape public outcomes.

To state this secular liberal view bluntly, religion and its ideological equivalents must be kept in the closet. Individuals may decide to participate in communities based on authorities that are not generally accessible. But such individuals should not expect their private preferences to determine public policies.

At a time when we hear so much from right-of-center political figures—whether they are Tea Party Republicans in the United States, louder conservative voices in much of Europe, or the governing coalition in Japan—it is worth remembering that this secular liberal view has been dominant in much of the world in recent decades. While fervent conviction can indeed emerge in ideologically fueled mass movements, it has more typically found expression privately or in small, supportive communities. As for the United States, more public testimony and larger-scale evangelism have at times been prominent in our history. But even with the growth in influence of the so-called Christian Right, the more characteristic pattern has been one of reticence in imposing particular religious views on the broader public.

In his very different setting three generations ago, William Butler Yeats captured our situation in his poem "The Second Coming": "The best lack all conviction, while the worst / Are full of passionate intensity." For Yeats as for us, "conviction" is a telling word. Its Latin stem means to overcome, to conquer, to be victorious. "Conviction" is the state of being persuaded, convinced—convicted in the sense of having any doubts rebutted. Yet "conviction" also refers to the act of finding someone guilty of an offense, convicted of a crime. So the word connotes confidence, certainty, and corroboration of views that opponents dispute. But the word is deployed to identify perpetrators of what is taken to be evil as often as it is used to designate advocates of worthy causes.

At a time when terrorism has become so salient a threat, it is hard to argue against any attempt to keep passionate conviction under whatever control is available. Yet as attractive as the plea for tolerance may be, it cannot appeal only to virtues of openness to all views and acceptance of multiple perspectives. Instead, any viable response to our current challenges must also be prepared to acknowledge, engage, and appraise the core values that animate and motivate all parties to its controversies.

This requirement accepts the fact that more than one perspective may be worthy of attention. It therefore rejects any claim to exclusive truth without further debate that allows appeal to generally accessible authorities. At the same time, this approach recognizes the extent to which personal convictions not only express private preferences but also legitimately influence public policies.

To return to Yeats's poetic formulation, neither a lack of all conviction nor an overflow of passionate intensity is adequate. Passionate intensity alone does not settle the matter, if only because there are multiple candidates who can base their claim on this consideration. And the lack of all conviction is not only unfair as a characterization of secular liberal pleas for tolerance but is also in any case incapable of holding its own against passionate intensities.

## The Need for Comparative Appraisal

The imperative that results from this standoff calls for a more robust public appraisal of views that many in the West for too long have relegated to the status of private preferences. We all know that personal convictions have social ramifications. We can no longer afford the luxury of pretending that is not the case even if the alternative is less comfortable than an ethos that simply tolerates any and all positions.

In an age of increased global awareness, this need for more robust public appraisal is all the more acute. Appeals to allegedly absolute authorities somehow are less dispositive or immediately compelling in the face of competing claims that seem similarly grounded. The invocation of inerrant texts loses some of its punch when the Bible of the fundamentalist Christian confronts the Qur'an of the Wahhabi Muslim or the *Pāli Canon* of the Theravāda Buddhist. The retreat to inaccessible private experience—"You just have to know Jesus"—is less overwhelming as a strategy when it encounters the very similar approaches of other pietistic and mystical traditions.

The processes captured in the buzzword "globalization" press us toward a comparative perspective that entails public attention to what otherwise might remain private. This comparative perspective is almost unavoidably critical and at its best is also self-critical. As we become aware of comparability among ostensibly quite disparate communities, we also cannot help noticing the enormous variety within nominally unified traditions. This variety is evident historically: even the most stable traditions change over time. But there are also great differences even at a single point of time—including, of course, the present.

This variety is evident in Christian and Jewish communities both over time and in the present. Consider fourth-century Catholicism in North Africa, fifteenth-century Christian Orthodoxy in Constantinople, and eighteenth-century Deism in England. Or recall an Evangelical Baptist and a high-church Episcopalian whom you may know. Or think of the enormously rich and diverse streams of Jewish tradition simplified as Orthodox, Conservative, and Reform.

Similar and if anything even more variety is evident in Hindu and Buddhist communities. In the case of what we homogenize as Hinduism, the diversity is all the more remarkable because it developed for most of its history within the single (admittedly large and variegated) country of India. In contrast, Buddhists moved out from India across Asia and more recently to Europe and the Americas and developed a virtually limitless array of permutations and combinations with other traditions. In particular in China and Japan, Buddhists have blended their beliefs and practices and more or less amicably lived side by side with Confucian, Taoist, and Shinto traditions.

Along with Buddhism and Christianity, Islam is the third great missionary religion in human history, and it too has become rooted in a remarkable range of cultures. Islam has resisted complete indigenization, in particular through its refusal to allow the Qur'an to be invoked liturgically in any language other than Arabic. Yet there is still great diversity in Islam, far more than is suggested by the frequent tendency in the West to identify it almost exclusively with the Arabian Peninsula. After all, Indonesia has the largest Muslim population in the world, and India has the largest Muslim minority of any country. And, as has become urgently evident in recent years, even within the Arabian Peninsula and the Middle East there is the considerable diversity and tension that the division between Sunni and Shia communities represents.

## Public Religion and Self-critical Secularism

All of this diversity within various religious traditions calls attention to a fact too easily overlooked in periods when the prevailing ethos calls for tolerance: religious people themselves almost never deem their convictions to be private preferences that can be divorced from deliberations about public policies. Instead, they engage in vigorous debate among themselves as to the most adequate understanding of their shared traditions because they believe it to be of utmost importance to be right in their convictions. And they are also prepared to be public advocates for what their convictions imply for society as a whole.

At a time of social antagonisms that are in part religiously based, this public face of religion is perhaps unwelcome. Surely the world would be safer if such fervent convictions were kept out of the public square. But this option, so attractive to secular liberalism, is—to repeat—simply not acceptable to those whose deepest convictions would be relegated to the status of private preferences without any relevance to public policy.

As challenging as is the insistent presence of religion and its ideological equivalents in public life, it also represents a great opportunity. Recognition of disagreements within a nominally unified tradition opens the door to self-criticism. This process is in fact always under way. But greater awareness of it can encourage support that allows muted, minority, or suppressed views to be voiced with greater vigor.

An example of this encouragement that is especially attractive to the West at the moment is the call for proponents of moderate Islam to become more vocal over against their extremist coreligionists. There certainly are such moderate voices: Muslims who affirm *jihad* as the struggle to live faithfully, who exemplify peaceful coexistence with non-Muslims, who reject suicide bombing and other forms of terrorism. As in other religious communities, there is always a contest underway for the right to claim the designation "Muslim." This internal contest should not, however, obscure the extent of common ground across a great range of Muslims in opposition to prevailing trends in the West. Indeed, in this respect Muslims also speak for large numbers of religiously serious adherents to other traditions.

Here we return again to the contrast between passionate intensity and lack of all conviction. Even those of the religiously committed who oppose exclusionist extremism and hostility to all outsiders are often strongly critical of what they see as the corrosive individualism and secularism of the West. Passive accommodation to the hedonism and materialism of secular Western culture is in this view to lack all conviction. The sense of such accommodation in turn generates further support for the passionate intensity that the most extreme positions represent.

Just as we encourage debate within the Muslim world, we must therefore also welcome vigorous criticism of prevailing trends in the West. Only if we resist our own tendencies to provincialism and triumphalism will we be able to acknowledge, engage, and evaluate the multiple streams in our own traditions. And on that basis, we can perhaps also recognize points of contact with the very different perspectives of outsiders who criticize and even attack us. Paradoxically, we can more effectively engage the opposition we generate if we are willing to address social patterns deplored not only by those who attack us but also by vast numbers of others, including even many of our friends and allies around the world.

## Individualism and Western Liberalism

Perhaps the most central instance of those patterns is the celebration of individualism without adequate attention to the communities it presupposes. This tendency is often reinforced with vigorous advocacy for unfettered markets and unimpeded capital flows. Indeed, *laissez-faire* capitalism is frequently presented as integral to the traditions of individual freedom that in turn elicit much of the convinced antagonism to secular Western culture.

The flaws of individualism as it is represented in modern Western free-market ideology and mass culture are evident even when current patterns are evaluated in terms of their own historical antecedents. Central to this patrimony are the powerfully influential figures of John Locke and Adam Smith in Britain and Immanuel Kant on the Continent. Yet none of these thinkers provides support for the kind of uncritical individualism that characterizes the rhetoric of so many of those who presently invoke their names.

As a matter of historical fact, Locke—notably in his *Letters on Toleration* (1690, 1693) and in the second of his *Two Treatises of Civil Government* (1690)—certainly gave considerable impetus to the traditions that have come to characterize the political and economic orientation of Western liberal democracy. In particular, his second *Treatise* delineates his view of humanity in the state of nature. Arguing against the position of Thomas Hobbes that humans originate in a state of hostility and antagonism, Locke envisions equal and independent individuals who enjoy a natural happiness. Yet even though he is far more positive about human nature than is Hobbes, Locke too moves quickly to the formation of the state as a means of protection against the excesses of individualism. Thus the social contract is required to guard against any who might attempt to live outside the law of nature.

Like Locke, Kant is appropriately counted among those who have shaped modern Western individualism. His central concern to preserve human freedom and moral autonomy while also acknowledging the power of scientific understanding places him squarely in this tradition. Indeed, his preoccupation with establishing a solid foundation for personal moral agency and responsibility in the impersonal world of modern science is emblematic for Western individualism, even among those who have scarcely heard of him and who certainly are not aware of the intellectual revolution that his thought constitutes.

Yet, like Locke, Kant is far from advocating an uncritical individualism. Knowledge, for Kant preeminently exemplified in Newtonian physics, can never be a matter of individual idiosyncrasy but rather must be universal and necessary. Similarly, moral action—reason in its practical employment, to put it in terms of his conceptual apparatus—presupposes a shared context of meaning and common criteria for adjudicating alternatives. (In Kant's technical terminology, the postulates of practical reason constitute the shared context of meaning and the categorical imperative in its various formulations specifies the criterion for determining which actions are moral.) This embedding of attention to human freedom and moral autonomy in more inclusive contexts is integral to the analyses of the *Critique of Pure Reason* (1781) and the *Critique of Practical Reason* (1788). But it becomes ever more central in Kant's later writings: the *Critique of Judgment* (1790), *Religion Within the Limits of Reason Alone* (1793), and in such pieces as the extended essay *Perpetual Peace* (1795).

Like Locke and Kant, Adam Smith is appropriately enlisted in the cause of Western individualism. His thought also represents the close historical connection between this tradition of individualism and modern Western *laissez-faire* economic theory. Yet what Smith actually wrote lends little support to the more recent arguments for unconstrained markets and unrestrained individualism on behalf of which his name is so often invoked.

In his *An Inquiry into the Nature and Causes of the Wealth of Nations* (1776), Smith certainly contends that the individual pursuit of self-interest can contribute to the public good and general welfare. But he also recognizes that the ambitions of individuals and private groups might be opposed to the public interest and in such cases would require restrictions imposed by the state. More fundamentally, Smith, who was a professor of moral philosophy, affirms the pursuit of individual interests only in the context of a network of social relations, as is clearly articulated in his *Theory of Moral Sentiments* (1759).

## Religion and Individualism

In affirming the role of the community in constraining the excesses of individual self-assertion, Locke, Kant, and Smith all in effect stand with the vast preponderance of human wisdom and experience over against only the modern West that so often invokes their names.

Perhaps the most radical insight into the inadequacy of idealization of the individual is the position of Buddhist traditions that there is no self. This teaching of *anattā* or *anātman* is shared across a remarkable range of Buddhist communities, from Theravāda traditions in South and Southeast Asia, to their Mahāyāna counterparts in East Asia, and to all of their offspring in the West. To construe the self as an individual entity is to fail to apprehend the codependence of all of reality. It is to be captive to an illusion and therefore to live in delusion.

Other religious traditions express this same position in various ways. Traditions as disparate as Confucianism on the one hand and Judaism and Islam on the other deem individuals to be constituted through their social relationships. In short, for Confucians, Jews, and Muslims, the community has logical, temporal, and normative priority over the individual.

Even those religious conceptions that seem to glorify the individual in the end subordinate the self to a more encompassing normative structure or reality. I offer two examples. The Hindu affirmation that *atman* is *brahman*—that the self is identical with the ultimate—does celebrate the dignity of the human person. But for Hindus this equation precisely does not exalt the discrete individual as separate from the undifferentiated whole of which it is an integral part. A second example is the Greek and then Christian idea of the soul. This conception confers enduring worth on the individual and, unlike the Hindu affirmation of *atman*, it does not dissolve this individual into the ultimate. Yet even when the soul is construed as an enduring individual entity, its end is to love, to enjoy, and to worship the divine reality for which it is destined.

## The Challenge of Inclusive Community

Unconstrained individualism and feebly regulated markets not only reinforce each other but in combination also support perverse tendencies that must instead be resisted. To note two instances, this combination powerfully encourages trends both toward wider gaps between the top and the bottom of the distribution of income and wealth and toward the elevation of private interests over public goods. These trends lead to increased burdens on those least able to bear them. But beyond the deprivation of individuals, the single most negative institutional result of this confluence of impacts is the systematic undermining of any positive conception for the role of communities at all levels, from families and neighborhoods to voluntary associations, governments, and even multinational organizations.

While the processes captured in the term "globalization" certainly can serve to accentuate these perverse trends, greater global integration may also point in another direction. This other direction is already indicated in both the overwhelming preponderance of the testimony of the major world religions and in the admonitions of central thinkers in the tradition of Western liberalism like Locke, Kant, and Smith. The goal toward which this alternative points is a sense of increasingly inclusive community that focuses attention and concentrates investments on the imperative of including the vast numbers of people who so far have been excluded from the benefits of globalization.

This goal of an inclusive global community is no doubt very far in the future. Indeed, developments of recent decades have resulted in its receding even further into the distance. Consequently moving toward the goal requires a basic change in orientation, not simply further steps in the direction we are already going. In particular, we must shift away from our exclusive preoccupation with markets and individuals.

Despite their differences on a host of issues, Locke, Kant, and Smith agree on the role of community or the broader society in constraining individual self-assertion. To repeat, in this respect they join in the virtually unanimous testimony of the world's religious traditions. The challenge then is to integrate this imperative with the dynamism of modern secular economic life—a challenge that can be met only if public goods are valued along with the productive capacity of private interests.

Rising to this abstractly stated challenge in concrete ways will require a host of public policy initiatives. In terms of domestic priorities, the United States in particular must shift fundamentally from proposals that disproportionately favor the very top stratum of society to programs that redress the escalating gap between the rich and the poor. In the American context, that means support for legislation like the earned income tax credit and a rejection of tax cuts that indefensibly benefit the wealthiest citizens. In the international arena, what is called for are rounds of trade agreements that in fact deliver on preferences for the poorest countries and increased aid that targets people and communities ready, willing, and able to move forward on the basis of their own efforts as those efforts are stimulated and reinforced through foreign assistance.

I will not pretend to lay out a full agenda of legislative proposals for either domestic or international programs. But the shift from the approach of the recent past could not be sharper. Instead of initiatives that favor the already privileged, we must move toward policies designed to enlist the promise of globalization for the promotion of a worldwide community that benefits not only the rich but also the poor.

## Conviction in the Context of Inclusive Community

An approach to globalization that breaks with uncritical adulation of private interests over public goods, of markets over governments, and of the individual over the community also affords the prospect of reconsidering the character of conviction in the context of inclusiveness. Globalization need not entail acceptance of Western secularism to the exclusion of the traditions of other communities. Precisely because some societies have developed ways of appreciating diversity and allowing participation in a shared polity even among those who in other respects disagree on basic issues, the goal of inclusive community does not require cultural or religious homogeneity.

The achievement of such multicultural or pluralistic societies is certainly fragile. In some cases, particular convictions of those "full of passionate intensity" flare up with horrible consequences, as in the occasional eruptions of violence over holy sites in India or the vicious attacks on Muslims in Myanmar. In other cases, relative tranquility is maintained in significant part because large segments of the population are more or less indifferent—having what might be called a "lack [of] all conviction"—as in much of Western Europe. But the fact remains that large-scale societies have been able to develop social institutions and cultural mores that support an inclusive community. In this sense an ordered social system has allowed space for the convictions of more than one particular community to be expressed.

As the examples of India and Western Europe suggest, the context for this pluralism or multiculturalism is often a relatively secular society that offers a stable setting for the expression of diverse traditions. But that need not be the case. Even in the instances of India and Western Europe, the setting is certainly not neutral, as is evident from the historical dominance of Hindu and Christian traditions respectively. China offers another pattern: Confucian, Taoist, and Buddhist traditions have coexisted in a considerable range in the orientation of governmental authorities. Yet another example is the interaction of Buddhist, Shinto, and other traditions in Japan.

This historical variety is significant because it calls attention to the need to resist a provincialism that might take any one situation to be normative. This orientation might, for example, assume that modern global and predominantly Western social and cultural patterns constitute the default setting within which more particular communities may be able to flourish. But this assumption is problematic not only because of its unacknowledged provincialism but also because its disregard of the extent to which the interactions between particular communities and the larger society can be effective in both directions.

Especially for those individuals and communities that are vehemently opposed to the dominant patterns of the secular West, it is crucial that the prospect of change in prevailing tendencies not be foreclosed. Here antagonists of the West and opposition from within may share common ground, even if there is no overt collaboration. The consumer society and mass culture that the West in general and the United States in particular have produced invites vigorous criticism.

This mix of consumer society and mass culture too often seems to be little more than a social system minus any ethical or normative grounding. Insofar as this combination of social and cultural patterns indeed represents what critics deem to be a passive accommodation to the hedonism and materialism of secular Western tendencies, it cries out for a reconnection to the roots of the more particular communities. Such communities may be grounded in a substantial range of traditions—religious, ethnic, cultural, educational, political, vocational. In each case, these communities affirm internal norms that guide their shared practice. This pattern is most readily recognizable in religious communities, especially if they represent a minority within the larger society. But it is also evident in other voluntary associations, whether ethnic, cultural, educational, or political. It may also be realized in professional or vocational associations, in which definite values or commitments—sometimes formally articulated, at other times only tacit—govern standard or acceptable behavior and frequently also energize participants to exertions that far exceed any ordinary occupational requirements.

What such particular communities have in common is more or less a self-conscious resistance to accepting the conventional patterns of the prevailing culture as adequate to their own deepest convictions. Put positively, such communities hold out the promise of a richer, fuller social system that affirmatively incorporates community within it. A society so ordered would be a worthy achievement of globalization and could rightly claim to be an example of inclusive community.

# PART 1

*Education as a Resource*

# 2 The Challenges of American Provincialism

EDUCATION IS AN INDISPENSABLE resource for any quest for more inclusive communities because of the need to engage the longstanding but ever more counterproductive provincialism at the heart of so much of American public life.

## American Provincialism

For most of our history, we in the United States have been subject to the charge of provincialism. In its formative years, the United States was far removed from the then centers of world influence. The frontier mentality of a population pressing into new territory also did not lend itself to cosmopolitanism. And the enormous size of the country once we expanded our borders to the full breadth of the continent allowed a self-contained preoccupation with the domestic as distinguished from international concerns.

Despite this long-established pattern of self-containment and distance, the twentieth century, as we are all very much aware, witnessed the emergence of the United States initially as one international force among others and by the end of the century as indisputably the world's preeminent global power. Yet, despite its global reach, the United States has continued to exhibit its entrenched tendency to go its own way. To take one striking instance, when President Woodrow Wilson pressed a visionary international agenda, Congress—with the opposition led by Senator Henry Cabot

An initial version of this chapter was given as a talk in January 2007 to a gathering of senior university administrators under the auspices of the Council of Independent Colleges.

Lodge (R-MA)—refused to authorize U.S. membership in the League of Nations because of concerns that joining would compromise American independence of action. The pattern illustrated in the antagonism between Wilson and Lodge is repeated again and again during the course of the twentieth century. But there is no need to multiply historical examples here; in a sense both the global role and the insistence on independence have reached as high a level as at any previous time in the first decade and a half of the twenty-first century.

In its declaration of a right to preemptive action and its early disdain for multilateral institutions and processes, the administration of President George W. Bush maintained both its indispensability to global order and its independence of the constraints that bind other countries. This position is advanced in rhetoric that is remarkably provincial in its projection of American exceptionalism, even as it claims to formulate principles that are universal. In this sense the rhetoric accurately expresses the double claim to independence and indispensability.

To put it mildly, this position did not earn plaudits abroad. More bluntly, the combination of arrogance and ignorance resulted in the virtual collapse of American standing around the world. Those of us who have spent considerable time overseas in recent decades can report with certainty that the United States had seldom if ever been held in such low esteem as in the early years of this century, not only in Europe but also in the Middle East, Asia, Africa, and Latin America.

While negative views of the United States no doubt also reflect such less admirable qualities as envy and resentment, the decline in our international standing in the first years of the twenty-first century is in significant part the consequence of an extended series of bad judgments. These judgments are more often than not a product of insufficient knowledge, a lack of curiosity, or an incapacity to view issues from more than one perspective; of an unquestioning assumption that everyone the world over admires Americans; or of an uncritical presumption that our position is right and good. I would applaud mightily if our colleges and universities could guarantee that such mistakes would never again be made! But I propose that we focus instead on a more tractable challenge that our colleges and universities have substantial resources to address—namely, the provincialism that too often shapes our public policy deliberations.

I would be surprised if I have to document the extent of this provincialism even on our campuses. But in case there are any doubts, I will refer briefly to three recent reports. Here are a few of the findings.

From a National Geographic survey of Americans in the 18–24 age group:

- Almost 30 percent thought the population of the United States amounted to 1 to 2 billion people.
- 11 percent could not locate the United States on a world map.
- Only one in seven could find Iraq or Iran on a map of the Middle East and Asia; for locating Saudi Arabia, the figure was 24 percent; for Israel, 14 percent.
- On a world map, only 17 percent could find Afghanistan and only 19 percent could locate Germany.
- Only 25 percent could identify China and India as the two countries with populations of more than a billion people.

From a recent Asia Society survey:

- 25 percent of college-bound high school students did not know the name of the ocean that separates the United States from Asia.
- 80 percent did not know that India is the world's largest democracy.

From a recent American Council on Education report:

- Fewer than 1 percent of American graduate students are studying languages deemed by the U.S. government as critical to national security.
- Approximately 25 percent of K–12 schools that are seeking to hire foreign language teachers are unable to find them.

I suspect, of course, that all of us deem the students who attend the colleges and universities with which we most identify to be much more sophisticated and cosmopolitan than the provincials whose knowledge is recorded in these surveys and reports. I certainly hope that is the case. But even if it is, all of our colleges and universities have an opportunity to build from whatever foundation is in place toward the framework we need if the United States is going to play a constructive global role.

## Developing Faculty and Curricular Resources

This building process must begin with the basic instruction in language and culture that even many of our best students—and faculty—all too frequently lack. To learn about other languages and cultures may seem self-evident at a time of accelerating interaction on a global scale. Yet the fact that we live in an increasingly integrated world in which the United States exercises enormous global influence may paradoxically serve to undermine this focus on the fundamentals of other languages and cultures.

We have all heard endlessly about globalization. We live in a world that is ever more insistently connected, over previously almost unimaginable distances. We are acutely aware of our unprecedented situation: more extensive international media; less expensive transportation and communication; the explosion of e-mail and the Internet; increasingly efficient transfers of money, goods and services, ideas and intellectual or cultural property of all kinds, and even people across any and all borders.

The paradox is that these powerful processes of globalization may fuel the illusion that it will be enough if our students and faculty understand this increasingly integrated world through a U.S.-dominated perspective. All that is needed in this view is an array of courses and faculty to teach them in such areas as global finance, international relations, development economics, world literature, and comparative cultures. Those are the specializations appropriate for colleges and universities aware of the new global reality that shapes us all.

I appreciate and applaud such courses. I have even taught some with titles that include terms like "comparative cultures," and I urge support for faculty and courses along these lines. Certainly the United States would be markedly less provincial if every graduate of our higher education system had at least a few courses that exemplify such awareness of globalization.

And to get to that point is in itself a major challenge that will require substantial resources.

Still, as important as such courses are, the learning they impart also requires serious engagement with the particular languages and cultures that are compared or, worse, are homogenized into a global world culture that has English as its preferred language. Not every student needs to be closely acquainted with the other traditions that are incorporated into a globalized view. But if there is no deeply grounded knowledge of those other traditions, the danger is that we will assimilate them into our own views and erroneously assume that we have understood them.

Rather than presume that the world is more or less like us—or, at least in its heart of hearts, wants to be like us—we must do the hard work of learning about others who are different from us. And this imperative is not confined to the patent need for us to know more about the Middle East and the Muslim world. Clearly the world's largest countries, China and India, pose a stark contrast to us and will play a major role on the global stage in the decades and centuries ahead. So too will the current plight and the future prospects of sub-Saharan Africa affect us all, as will our neighbors in Central and South America, who are once again becoming vocal in their disenchantment with our high-handed dealings and dismissive stance toward them. Even apparently so similar Europe is more and more vigorously asserting its distinction from U.S. economic, political, and cultural values.

The challenge of learning about our neighbors around the world is a daunting one. Certainly it will require a division of labor! While no one can hope to understand the full variety of cultures worldwide, each of us should play a part. And if any institutions should take the lead in assembling an ensemble, if not a full orchestra of players, it is our colleges and universities.

Yet how many of our institutions of higher learning still have a language requirement for graduation? In how many languages do we provide instruction? I recognize that it is soberingly expensive to mount courses in a full range of languages, including ones spoken by only small numbers of people. Maybe not the Central African language of Bangando. Maybe not Mongolian. Maybe not even Thai or Croatian. But can we claim to offer an education adequate for the twenty-first century if we do not make available instruction in Chinese and Arabic and perhaps also Russian, Japanese, and Swahili in addition to usual options of French and Spanish? Many colleges and universities may find it advisable to participate in consortia so that a fuller range of offerings is available at an affordable cost. But by whatever arrangements, our educational institutions cannot execute their core responsibilities if we do not undertake to counter American provincialism as embodied in our students and our communities.

Language courses are of course only the tip of the iceberg—or better yet, the base of the mountain—of the instructional resources required. For an earlier generation, so-called "area studies" offered one approach to allowing at least minimal coverage of regions seldom examined in depth. With the decline in government resources for area studies, many of these programs have become smaller or have even been discontinued. But the challenge remains to provide curricula in the history and contemporary economic, political, and cultural life of nations around the world.

In response to this challenge European and American institutions of higher education are stunning in their continuing provincialism. In leading South Korean, Japanese, Chinese, Indian, African, or Latin American universities, it is unimaginable that the natural sciences or philosophy or economics would be taught without some reference to Western European and American materials. Even social sciences other than economics, as well as history and literature, include references to Western European and American parallels at a quite early stage. In contrast, American and European educational approaches too often refer to other traditions only in passing, as a special side interest, or at a very advanced stage of study.

As one who has invested decades in working for change in higher education, I certainly appreciate how difficult it is to respond to this challenge of moving toward a more globally responsible curriculum. I will not pretend to resolve all of the tough implementation issues. But I do insist that all of us who care about this country and are in positions of leadership in colleges and universities or other similar institutions must address the fact of American provincialism in every way we can.

## Cultivating Global Students

I realize that the curricular issues I have raised require tough choices among competing priorities and almost endless deliberations with the appropriate faculty bodies. I will not claim to assess the pros and cons of the tradeoffs that I know each institution will have to make. But I do have one strategy that I would like to commend in grappling with this set of issues. It has to do with one of the variables in the equation that always needs to be solved. That variable is the students at the heart of the education offered.

In regard to this variable I have two recommendations. The first is to diversify the student body as much as is feasible. The second is to facilitate a semester or preferably a year of study abroad for all students.

The first recommendation has received substandard attention in recent decades. Even so I note this recommendation anyway, and call attention in particular to its educational significance for the entire campus community. It is an important objective in its own right to offer educational opportunity to all prospective students. But beyond opening the doors of our colleges and universities to a broad range of applicants so that those too often excluded can benefit from higher education, having a diversity of students is itself a resource for countering provincialism. To be maximally beneficial, this diversity should include a significant range in terms of the income and ethnicity of American students and also a substantial contingent of international students from a broad array of countries and regions.

To have a curriculum that includes attention to minority perspectives in this country and is as full as is feasible a representation of non-American traditions is a crucial educational resource. But having colleagues who embody in person those other perspectives and traditions is an invaluable way to ensure that even students whose coursework moves in other directions will confront personalities and positions that are different from prevailing American views. Consequently, the educational opportunity is not only for the minority or international students but also for their classmates and the faculty, who of course also need to become more diverse.

As crucial as it is to attract a diverse student body to our campuses and to provide a cosmopolitan curriculum for their education, even the best execution of this responsibility still labors within the limitation of location in a more or less provincial American community. I know of no better way to counter that limitation than to encourage our students to study abroad for at least a semester and preferably a year. To facilitate such study abroad—for undergraduates, for graduate students, and for faculty—should be a priority for individual institutions and for American society as a whole, as represented in such government programs as the Fulbright Program and such nonprofit organizations as the Institute of International Education.

I can testify from personal experience that devoting substantial time to living and learning in another country offers an unparalleled opportunity for understanding not only another complex of traditions but also what is at the core of our own deepest commitments.

This point was impressed forcefully on me during 1962–1963, the first time I lived abroad. It was my junior year in college. My parents were both immigrants from Germany—my father coming to the United States in 1930, my mother in 1937. I had learned German before English yet I had never been outside North America. My parents had also emigrated from culturally very different regions of Germany—the Black Forest in my father's case and the Rhineland for my mother. So my year of study there, which included multiple visits to relatives on both sides of the family, was personally very intriguing. I saw in effect two sides of my personality embodied in two sets of relatives, each of whom assured me that I looked and acted just like the parent that was from their side of the family. While I was growing up, I had no small amount of tension with my father. As I was about to depart for the year, my mother said to me that after I met my father's family, I would understand him for the first time. And she was right.

But I learned more than just a better understanding of my family's psycho-cultural dynamics. Growing up, I had been quite critical of some of the social patterns taken for granted in the United States, including in particular widely accepted racial prejudices. This critical stance toward the United States did not disappear during my time in Germany and traveling more broadly in Europe. But as I came to learn more about these other societies and in particular about Germany, I also became much more aware of what I valued in America—and why, for better or worse, I would always be a convinced American. (I continue to feel that way—though the first part of the twenty-first century strained that allegiance more than at any previous time.)

I will note one further example from my own living abroad, this time in 1969–1970 when my wife Nancy, our older daughter Kathy, and I lived in Kandy, Sri Lanka, which was then still called Ceylon. I was there to study Buddhism, in significant part because I was intrigued with how different it was from the Christianity I had known all my life. In the course of that year I came to appreciate the enormous varieties within Buddhist traditions. But I also learned an important lesson about how preconceived ideas can profoundly shape our perceptions both of ourselves and of others.

As I got to know Buddhist acquaintances better, I realized that they had a very definite view of what a Christian must believe. Christians, they insisted, subscribed to the beliefs that there was a God outside the world, who created and governed it, and that individuals had immortal souls. They were confident that Christians held these positions because these tenets constituted the beliefs that in their view most clearly distinguished Christianity from Theravāda Buddhism (the version of Buddhist tradition prevalent in Sri Lanka as well as Myanmar, Thailand, Cambodia, and parts of Vietnam). I considered myself a Christian, but I affirmed neither of these positions. Indeed, my views in regard to the questions of the existence of God as a being outside the world and of the immortality of the soul were more akin to some Buddhist views than to prevailing Christian ones. Facing this unanticipated situation, my Buddhist friends did not revise their view of what Christians must believe; rather, they informed me that, given my positions, I could not be a Christian.

I refer to these illustrations from my own experience to call attention to what I deem to be an enormous two-fold benefit of living abroad in a way that deeply engages local traditions and is not simply in an American enclave. On the one hand, we indisputably learn about the historical patterns and contemporary personal, social, and cultural experiences of traditions different from our own. On the other hand, we also attain a kind of bifocal vision that allows us to see our own core values and deepest commitments more clearly because our perception includes a comparative perspective.

I apologize for what may seem to be a self-indulgent focus on my own experience. I have recalled the first two times I lived abroad in the hope, even the confidence, that my experience will trigger similar memories in others of you. In any case, such personal experiences are what colleges and universities can and should facilitate through opportunities for research and study abroad.

## Conclusion: Another Look at American Provincialism

Developing greater depth in faculty and curricular resources devoted to a wide range of languages and cultures; increasing on-campus diversity, including robust representatives of international students and faculty; and enhancing opportunities for study abroad are three long-term strategic initiatives that our colleges and universities should pursue. All three will contribute to building educational quality. In addition, such initiatives will help to address the provincialism that plagues American public life.

Clearly our educational enterprise by itself cannot definitively address the problem of American provincialism. That will require a much broader social and cultural process, including basic political choices. But we should not underestimate the impact that focused educational interventions can achieve.

To illustrate the broader impact of learning about and living in a very different culture, I will refer to an example from my work with the International Rescue Committee. The IRC is an international relief and development organization with operations in over forty countries around the world. The IRC's biggest programs have been in Pakistan and Afghanistan, on the Thai–Myanmar border, in the Democratic Republic of Congo, in Sudan, and now in Syria and its neighbors. Typically the IRC enters a country in response to an emergency precipitated by a conflict and then remains for as long as it takes to revitalize uprooted individuals and communities. On average this takes about eight years, though it is now over fifteen years for the DRC, twenty-five for the Thai–Myanmar border, and over thirty for Pakistan and Afghanistan.

The IRC also works in the United States with displaced people who are admitted as refugees for resettlement here. We have a network of twenty-two resettlement offices around the country. But the office I would like to refer to by way of illustration of the deprovincializing power of living abroad is Salt Lake City.

I have visited all of our resettlement offices, but my time with our Salt Lake City colleagues is probably the most memorable. I was struck again and again by how all of the people I met—our staff, community supporters, and, most importantly, the resettled refugees themselves—remarked on how wonderfully welcoming Salt Lake City was to refugees. The positive testimonials came even from refugees who had had difficulties in other communities and therefore commented positively on their experience in Salt Lake City in comparison.

I confess that I was initially mystified to discover that Utah would be so hospitable to refugees, including many from Africa and Asia. But in conversations with my colleagues, we all came to the conclusion that what contributed to this welcoming attitude was the fact that so many residents of Salt Lake City had lived abroad for a year or two. While Salt Lake City is not as predominantly Mormon as the rest of Utah, about half the population are members of the Church of Jesus Christ of the Latter-day Saints, to use the official name of the Mormon church. Members often spend two years or so in missionary service, many times outside of the United States. Up to half of the population of Salt Lake City is therefore the Mormon equivalent of returned Peace Corps volunteers. Their time abroad instills in many of these Mormons a sympathetic appreciation of the challenges that resettled refugees experience, which in turn translates into a sense of welcome to these new Americans.

To repeat, the experience of studying abroad and, more generally, learning about traditions different from American ones will not by itself succeed in overcoming American provincialism. But such educational initiatives can certainly play a significant role. Accordingly, I urge all of our colleges and universities to accentuate this dimension of study, to provide the requisite intellectual and financial resources required, and to encourage all students to seize the opportunity to pursue this avenue out of our various provincialisms.

My urging this priority counts for far less than the fact that the aim is robustly supported by the premier American institution that for about a century has supported international educational exchange—the Institute of International Education. I have had the privilege of serving on the IIE board for twenty years, and I am an enthusiastic supporter of its core purposes. As the IIE advances toward its centennial in 2019, it is enlisting partners from across American society to increase the number of U.S. students and scholars who engage in serious study and research abroad. The goal is to move that number to roughly 600,000, which would represent a doubling from the figure in 2013—a little over a 10 percent increase each year.

At the heart of this effort must be our educational institutions. IIE is working to enlist at least one hundred colleges and universities in a pledge to significantly expand the numbers of their own students who study abroad. It is also working with high-school teachers to encourage raising the value of studying abroad at an earlier age than is often done, and it is galvanizing its own alumni network of those who have studied abroad for an advocacy campaign. But success will also require increased investments from government at all levels as well as from corporations and a broad spectrum of civil society.

As such efforts are broadened and developed, we can all hope and expect that American provincialism will be more vigorously challenged at all levels. The experience of refugees resettled in Salt Lake City is indeed encouraging. As more and more of us come to know quite diverse societies first-hand through living and studying abroad, we as a country may hope and expect to move from welcoming outsiders to our shores to also learning from others how our ideas may be enhanced and our practices improved.

# 3  Religion and the Academy— A Lover's Quarrell

RELIGIOUS COMMUNITIES all too often exemplify extremes of provincialism. Yet religious studies as an academic discipline can serve the cause of openness to multiple traditions. Examining the relationship of religion to the academy over the centuries in a single institution may offer a measure of specificity to what admittedly is a highly general set of issues. Because I know it well and because the role of religion there is long and complex, I will focus on Harvard University.

## The Study of Religion at Harvard: A Historical Survey

I will begin at the very beginning. From 1636, when it was established by vote of the General Court of the Massachusetts Bay Colony, Harvard had a commitment to educating religious leaders. In the words of an early brochure (published in 1643):

> After God had carried us safe to New England and wee had builded our houses, provided necessaries for our livelihood, rear'd convenient places for God's worship, and settled the civil government: One of the next things we longed for and looked after was to advance learning and perpetuate it to posterity; dreading to leave an illiterate ministry to the churches, when our present ministers shall lie in the dust.
>
> (*New England's First Fruits*)

---

This chapter draws on a lecture delivered at Harvard University in September 2006 at the invitation of the Committee on the Study of Religion.

This concern to continue the tradition of a learned ministry figured predominantly in the first decades of the college and is reflected, for example, in the first endowed professorship at Harvard, also the oldest in the country: the Hollis Professorship of Divinity, established in 1721.

In the early nineteenth century, a discreet graduate program in theology was developed, initially with the organization of an advanced program for ministerial candidates in 1811 and then with the establishment of the Divinity School in 1816. The relationship between the Divinity School and the broader university, with all of its ups and downs over the years, is one significant perspective from which to view the relationship between the study of religion and the humanities more broadly. But before considering that theme further, I will note four other important points in this synoptic overview of the study of religion at Harvard.

First is the establishment of a formal Ph.D. program in the Faculty of the Arts and Sciences. Then called the "History and Philosophy of Religion," it was initiated in 1934. Certainly there was substantial attention to religion in the arts and sciences over the preceding three centuries, but this program was the first instance at Harvard of formal graduate studies in religion as distinguished from theology.

The second of my further historical notes is the establishment of the Center for the Study of World Religions, which opened in 1960 following an anonymous donation given in 1957. While the endowment of the Center is technically part of the funds of the Divinity School, it has from its inception served as a bridge between the Faculties of Divinity and Arts and Sciences. In terms of financial arrangements, the Center's endowment includes funds that allow significant discretion for investments in the Arts and Sciences. In broader terms, the Center has attracted both students and scholars from around the world for historical and comparative study, especially those from outside Christian traditions. Any of us who have had the privilege of living and studying there know from our experience that such historical and comparative study is enormously enriched when it is complemented with personal interaction among Center residents who embody a variety of traditions.

A third point in this overview is the 1963 renaming of the Faculty of Arts and Sciences Ph.D. program as the more generic "Study of Religion," signaling the inclusion of historical and comparative study across traditions. The committee charged with overseeing this program also administers the Divinity School's Th.D. program and comprises equal numbers of Arts and Sciences and Divinity faculty members. This structural arrangement has cemented a significant bond that has kept Divinity and Arts and Sciences colleagues in contact over the years, in contrast to institutions in which the respective doctoral programs are administered through entirely separate arrangements.

A final point in this historical survey is the 1974 establishment of the undergraduate concentration in comparative religion. Harvard was much later than almost all other private American colleges in establishing a curricular option for undergraduates to concentrate their studies in religion. Indeed, it was later than many of the best public colleges and universities, despite concerns about the separation of church and state. Furthermore, even when Harvard did finally venture into allowing religion as an undergraduate focus of study, it did so very cautiously. The program was a concentration, not a major; it therefore did not warrant the creation of a department but rather could be administered by the existing Committee on the Study of Religion. The concentration was also in *comparative* religion, to register unambiguously that it would not be a vehicle for indoctrination in a single tradition. Even more remarkably, the initial faculty leader for the program was a "loaner": Richard R. Niebuhr would take a leave from his duties at the Divinity School to become the founding director of the undergraduate concentration, but his permanent appointment would remain at the Divinity School. (I have a perhaps more vivid sense of the oddity of this arrangement because I first returned to Harvard to teach at the Divinity School with the explicit understanding that my appointment was a five-year, dead-end arrangement, as Dick would be returning after three years, which would give me two further years to figure out what I might do next. The arrangement also accounts for why I left after only three years: I found dead-end appointments unattractive.)

## The Study of Religion vs. Theology

I hope this brief overview will suffice for a thumbnail sketch of the study of religion at Harvard over the last almost 380 years. It may be a reflection of our culture of narcissism that I have focused on more recent decades. Still, as crucial as a long-term historical perspective is for a fuller view not only of the past but also of the best ways forward, our current issues are ones that have taken shape in the last half century.

It is entirely appropriate to celebrate the vote of the Faculty of Arts and Sciences in 1963 to establish the Committee on the Study of Religion and to draw the Committee's membership jointly from the Faculty of Divinity as well as from its own ranks. The continuing role of this Committee both in doctoral education and in administering the undergraduate concentration in comparative religion has, to repeat, been helpful in resisting the split between religious studies and theological studies. (As exemplified, for example, at Yale in the almost entirely separate trajectories of the Divinity School and the Department of Religious Studies, the latter also founded in 1963.) But our celebration of the institutional arrangements here should not be without reservation.

While most of us have long given up on insisting on purity of motivation, the establishment of the Committee on the Study of Religion is surely a case of motives that were decidedly mixed. For the Divinity School, the joint committee was a way to seek academic legitimation for a suspect area of study, and to do so in a way that allowed the conferring of the Ph.D. rather than only the Th.D. at a time when other theological schools were awarding the Ph.D. for theological programs. At the same time, Arts and Sciences was able to acknowledge the study of religion as legitimate while still retaining exclusive control of the Ph.D. as well as of the undergraduate programs when the Concentration in Comparative Religion was established a decade later.

If we now move from a focus on developments at Harvard to patterns across higher education as a whole, we cannot but observe that the very jointness of the Committee on the Study of Religion reflects the underlying tensions between theological education and religious studies. Even though the stated intention of this structure is to ensure collaboration across what otherwise could be an unhelpful divide, the formulation of this goal presupposes the distinction. It is therefore worth examining the underlying contrast in a little more detail.

At its worst, the contrast degenerates into mutual stereotyping. These stereotypes have arisen primarily because of the concern of scholars in the historical and philological study of religious traditions to distinguish themselves from theological inquiry. The result has been a self-characterization of historical and philological scholarship as objective study of other religious traditions in their own right rather than for apologetic purposes. In this self-characterization is the implied and not infrequently also explicit contrast to traditional theology, which is suspect insofar as it combines the description of data with concern for the normative commitments of a particular religious community. In its sharpest form the contrast is, in short, between objective and value-free study on the one hand and ideologically determined apologetics on the other.

It is worth noting how recent and uncharacteristic in human history is a clear differentiation between theology and the historical and philological study of religion. In the West before the Enlightenment and throughout the histories of virtually all other traditions around the world, theologians or those in similar positions of intellectual responsibility were presumed to have such knowledge as was available or desirable concerning what has come to be understood as the study of religion. That there should be a separate scholarly guild to provide information about other religious traditions is an innovation of the Enlightenment in the West. Even more recent is the intention that this information should be objective, as distinguished from either serving the apologetic purposes of a specific religious community or debunking the pretensions of one tradition through unfavorable comparison to another.

Despite its relatively brief duration, a clear differentiation of the historical and philological study of religion from theology has been notably productive. The aim of accurately and systematically describing the religious traditions of others in principle apart from both apologetic and iconoclastic interests has contributed measurably to the philological and historical understanding of the data of religious history. Indeed, this study has often been at the forefront of cross-cultural understanding as Western universities have only gradually moved out of very provincial conceptions—especially of the humanities.

## Two Contributions of the Study of Religion to the Academy

In assaying the contributions of the study of religion to the academy, this serious engagement with traditions other than those of the West has been conspicuously significant. Especially in relatively small institutions, courses in Hindu, Buddhist, and Muslim traditions have been far more typical in religion departments than have courses in non-Western cultures in literature, history, or philosophy departments. Similarly, faculty appointments and research foci have been less provincial in religion than in other humanities departments.

This early interest in the value of studying traditions other than those of the West constitutes a contribution of the study of religion to the academy that few would dispute. If one accepts the stereotypical dichotomy between the study of religion and theology, this contribution seems clearly to accrue to the study of religion side of the ledger. But even at this admittedly superficial curricular level, the dichotomy is seriously misleading, since Christian missionary impulses animated much of the earliest phase of the careful study of other religious traditions.

At a more basic intellectual level, the engagement with non-Western traditions undermines the dichotomy between theology and the study of religion because it presses the entire enterprise toward normative questions that have received insufficiently careful study in the modern secular university. Historical study of developing traditions that interact with one's own almost unavoidably raises comparative questions about relative adequacy to an increasingly shared experience. This process works in both directions:

Appraisal is directed toward what is observed and also reflected back on the values of the observer. As a result, both our awareness of others and our self-understandings increasingly focus on the question of truth from a critical and comparative perspective.

This critical and comparative perspective provides the opportunity to question the conception of academic study as value-free inquiry as opposed to appealing to that very conception in an attempt to secure respectability for the study of religion. Put positively, the study of religion should aspire to become a model of responsible attention to normative questions. This attention to questions of meaning and value is potentially a further positive dimension to the relationship of the study of religion to the academy.

To play this constructive role, we must recognize that both theology and the study of religion are engaged in a critical and comparative process of inquiry. There is, to be sure, the limiting case of investigators who insist that they are only describing what they see and that they are interested neither in assessing what they describe nor in allowing it to impinge on their views. This orientation has contributed extensively to the accumulation of data about other traditions and in this regard is worthy of respect. But the stated intention of this approach, to understand another tradition on its own terms, may have the effect of refusing to entertain even the possibility of its truth. Of course, the further result may then be that the adequacy of the investigator's own views is simply presumed. Ironically, this uncritical stance toward one's own values and disinterest in the normative claims of others is not altogether unlike the position of theologians who focus only on commending their own views in comparison to the commitment of others.

To participate self-consciously and self-critically in two or more traditions as part of a more inclusive community of inquiry is to reject the presumed adequacy of one's own views. For the historian of religions— and certainly for the comparative historian of religions—the result is that study becomes fully cross-cultural when inquiry directed toward understanding the other also invites reexamination of one's own traditions. Similarly, for the theologian, exposition and advocacy of his or her own position cannot proceed on the basis of authorities simply presumed to be incommensurate with those of other communities and inaccessible to participants in other traditions.

## Religion Today: Both Vital and Contested

This view not only of the study of religion but also of theology as constructive participants in the humanities and the social sciences is starkly at odds with the conventional wisdom of the academy a mere generation ago. While the then prevailing view welcomed historical and philological studies, it more or less explicitly deemed religious affirmations or claims to be remnants of a soon-to-be overtaken traditionalism. In short, such affirmations or claims were vestiges of a past that would die out in the near future.

The intervening decades have not been supportive of this perspective. In the American context, first Jerry Falwell and the Moral Majority in the 1980s and then the more recent resurgence of Christian conservatives have demonstrated that religion can be a potent political force even in an affluent, pluralistic, and nominally secular country. At the same time the flourishing of often extremist Muslim, Hindu, and even Buddhist movements around the world has illustrated the remarkably resilient power of religion in the contemporary international scene.

The unexpected, and perhaps unwelcome or even undesirable, resurgence—or at least, the continuing vitality—of religion serves to underscore how crucial it is that both the study of religion and theology contribute effectively to the academy. Certainly academic inquiry by itself will not be able to account fully for the impact of religion on contemporary society. But understanding the religious traditions that inspire committed individuals and shape devout communities can still play an indispensable role in interpreting our world today.

Beyond understanding religious traditions is the imperative that we engage the challenge that extremist religions pose for the modern secular world. In this context, the comparative and critical enterprise that theological inquiry at its best represents is even more indispensable than the historical and philological study of religion. There can be no satisfactory interaction with the most relentless critics of the modern West unless the claims of what we deem to be extremist views are taken seriously. That means allowing encounters in which critics of the West are not required to accept in advance the premises of their antagonists. As a result, precisely the normative questions that have received insufficient careful study in the modern secular university must again become a focus of attention.

Here both comparative historians of religion and theologians can play a significant role—a role that is directly continuous with the two contributions I have previously identified: cultivating appreciation for non-Western traditions and recognizing a comparative dimension to normative questions. Historians of religion and increasingly also theologians recognize that traditions develop over time and that at any point in time there are multiple claimants for the authority of most adequately representing a nominally unified tradition. As a result, not only scholars but also adherents of a religious tradition are constantly engaged—whether or not they are aware of it—in a process of comparative appraisal.

The novelty of the contemporary situation should not be overstated. After all, awareness of differences among religious traditions on virtually every issue—including the question of how the ultimate is most appropriately conceived, addressed, or realized—is scarcely an unprecedented development. Within nominally unified communities, there have always been controversies among competing alternative interpretations of shared traditions. Similarly, conflict between clearly distinguished communities has been only too characteristic of the religious landscape over the centuries. But what is new is the increasingly widespread recognition both of substantial change over time within continuing communities and of systematic parallels in the development of traditions that are historically only remotely related.

Both changes within a continuing community and apparent similarities across distinct communities allow traditionalist interpretations. Change over time is in this case construed as a series of heretical deviations from what can be identified and must be affirmed as the strictly maintained standard of orthodoxy. Similarly, the impression of parallels in quite different traditions is resisted, because it is held to result from a comparison of positions that are, when rightly viewed, incommensurable. In the case of such traditionalist interpretations, increased awareness of both changes within and parallels between religious communities is resisted and in turn countered through reiterated appeals to an inerrant authority that guarantees unique truth.

This assertion of traditional authority continues to exercise impressive (and at times volatile) power, perhaps especially in the face of anxiety over changes within and parallels between communities. It cannot, however, alter the increasing recognition of the comparative context of such appeals. As I noted in the introduction, the Theravāda Buddhist who relies on the inerrant authority of the *Pāli Canon*, the fundamentalist Christian who bases his or her certainty on the verbally inspired Word of God, and the Wahhabi Muslim who cites the infallible Qur'an all may give each other pause—and the more so as they become aware of the extraordinarily impressive figures in their own traditions who have not shared their appeal to inerrantly authoritative, verbally inspired, and infallibly accurate texts. Similarly, appeals to supernatural events, precisely prescribed ritual practices, or incommunicable self-authenticating experiences have less self-evident authority as there is increased awareness of differing interpretations within a single community and intriguing parallels in other traditions.

## Religion, Comparative Appraisal, and the Academy

The effect of the historical and cross-cultural awareness is, then, frequently—even characteristically and, in the end, perhaps unavoidably—to call into question every appeal to a putatively inerrant authority. Awareness that has a comparative dimension, and in that comparison is not only appreciative but also critical and self-critical, in effect relativizes every such appeal. Diversity within a tradition renders problematical every sharply delineated standard of orthodoxy; comparison among communities invites appeal to considerations not confined to any one tradition. Thus, in practice even if not consistently in theory, the authority of any one tradition is subjected to appraisal on the basis of criteria that are arguably applicable over time and across traditions. The criteria on which such comparative appraisal is based are themselves subject to evaluation. There is a plurality of positions on the issue of how most adequately to construe those criteria. But however diverse may be the specific criteria employed, they are all expressions of the general recognition that appealing to the authority of tradition alone does not suffice.

Here again, the novelty of the contemporary situation should not be overstated. Even a cursory reading in the history of any religious community offers ample evidence that the truth of particular positions has been commended not only through appeals to traditional authorities but also through claims to illumine and in turn influence contemporary experience. References to tradition and either implicit or explicit claims to represent that tradition on the one hand and arguments about the capacity to interpret and shape life today on the other of course appear in greatly differing ratios. But both forms of appeal are almost always present. In Christian traditions, for example, the distinction between dogmatic and philosophical theology suggests poles between which there is a spectrum of approaches. Even in those traditions for which the designation "dogmatic" is invariably pejorative, there is still a combining of appeals to authoritative traditions and contemporary experience. Similarly, even the most insistently dogmatic theology at least tacitly claims to focus and clarify the ultimately crucial features of lived experience.

But while claims to illumine and influence contemporary experience have ample precedents in virtually all religious traditions, such claims have not been the focus of attention to the extent that they are when they are viewed in the context of increased awareness of changes within and parallels between communities. As this double awareness in effect relativizes the authority of tradition, it at the same time increases the force of claims to interpret and in turn shape the whole of human experience. As a result, the question of criteria for adjudicating the relative adequacy of such claims becomes an inescapable issue for theology and its counterparts in nontheistic traditions. These criteria must address the two sets of considerations implied in references not only to interpreting but also to shaping the whole of human experience—that is, the criteria must address both descriptive and normative adequacy.

To aspire to interpret the whole of human experience entails a commitment to comprehensiveness that precludes retreat into a private or even a socially and culturally provincial sphere. Standards of descriptive adequacy thus seek to measure the extent and the depth to which the symbolic resources of a tradition have the capacity to incorporate into that frame of reference any and every datum of experience. Included here are, of course, the perennial questions, crises, and transitions that all religious traditions address: the relationship of the human to the natural, the cosmic, the ultimate; the realities of evil and suffering, of compassion and liberation; the meaning of life itself from birth through the struggles and support of various communities to its end in individual and perhaps collective death. But also included are particular historical developments, such as the missionary success of Islam, the economic power of capitalism, techniques for family planning and organ transplants, and the threat of nuclear annihilation. The criterion of adequacy to experience measures the capacity to interpret the entire range of data through the symbolic resources of the tradition, a capacity that in turn requires the vitality to accommodate new insights not anticipated in the tradition itself.

Important as is the capacity to interpret all of life, this descriptive adequacy is incomplete apart from its normative dimension. Indeed, mutual assessment of religious positions probably more often than not focuses on this dimension of implications for shaping the world. What is the hierarchy of values presupposed in religious positions that take the goal of religious discipline or devotion to be deliverance to a realm or an existence sharply distinguished from life in space and time? What are the consequences of construing the individual self as an illusion, or as an infinitely valuable personality with an eternal destiny, or as only provisionally discrete from the ultimate reality of which it is an expression? What is the impact on human being and value of trust in a deity who governs the whole of history, or of commitment to a moral order that elicits fervent obedience, or of insight into the ultimate emptiness of all reality?

Interaction among traditions that includes both comparative understanding and at least tacit mutual appraisal will not, of course, reach easy or early agreement on judgments of relative descriptive and normative adequacy. Indeed, the least likely of the benefits of such interaction is any anticipated agreement. But what may and will occur is an acceleration of the ongoing process of development within each of the communities involved. For example, members of a community may discover that their tradition has attended insufficiently to the implications of astronomy, physics, or genetics in its representation of the human condition and may, therefore, seek to take those data more thoroughly into account. Others may work to develop new emphases to counteract traditional tendencies toward tolerating or even legitimating social inequities that on reflection they are not prepared to affirm. Still others may conclude that the insistent iconoclasm of their traditions requires rethinking in view of the beauty of painting and sculpture evident in other communities but proscribed from theirs.

Such interaction and change do not require prior agreement on criteria for mutual appraisal. Instead, members of the various communities may bring to the process quite different and perhaps very particular criteria for assessing descriptive and normative adequacy. Differences in the criteria employed are not, however, disabling insofar as the initial and probably most crucial outcome of the process is change in one's own position. For in the case of such reflexive change, the criteria guiding this process are precisely the ones that are compelling to those who are modifying or developing their own positions.

This focus on reflexive change is a third contribution of the study of religion not only to the humanities but also to the encounter of the modern West with religious conviction worldwide. What makes this encounter especially explosive is the sense on the part of religiously committed individuals and communities that the standpoint of the secular West is not prepared to engage any other perspectives on their own terms. To open up the prospect of change in their own positions on the part of all participants is a major advance beyond the current standoff. For those citizens of the West—in particular, for those members of the academy—who are critical of major trends in modern Western secular society, this openness to self-criticism and reflexive change is in any case welcome. But it furthermore affords an opportunity for constructive encounters with self-proclaimed antagonists.

To summarize, there are at least three contributions of the study of religion to the humanities and therefore to the academy and the larger world. First, both theology and the study of religion at their best have played a historically significant role in serious engagement with non-Western traditions. Second, both theology and the study of religion at their best have insisted on addressing normative issues even when the prevailing ethos of the academy has focused almost exclusively on descriptive concerns. Third, both theology and the study of religion at their best have pressed the case for comparative appraisal that allows for self-criticism as well as a critique of the positions of others.

I submit that this three-fold contribution provides ample warrant for the housing of the study of religion (including theology) in every college or university, certainly including Harvard.

# 4 Universities in the Search for Strategic Responses to Global Challenges

EDUCATION HAS A crucial role to play in preparing the next generation for participation in inclusive communities. To perform that role, universities must grapple with major challenges to their viability in an era when educational resources are offered over the Internet virtually free. In interestingly analogous ways, Japanese and American institutions prove how fundamental those challenges are.

Only if the core requirements of sufficient funding and well-prepared students in adequate numbers are available can universities in even the wealthiest countries execute this task of educating the next generation of leaders. It is therefore worth examining the prospects for such institutions in the current conflicted situation in both Japan and the United States. Precisely because the situation in these two countries is so different in so many ways, unexpected lessons may be learned for institutions in one based on responses to these challenges in the other.

The challenges that Japanese and American universities face are straightforward—and, regrettably, quite fundamental. I will focus on three basic ones: first, the numbers and quality of our students; second, the sources and scale of our funding; and third, the institutional identity that stems from our heritage and shapes our prospects. These three challenges are certainly interconnected but can still be usefully distinguished.

---

An initial version of this chapter was given as a talk at the invitation of the Japan University Accreditation Association (JUAA) in Tokyo in September 2013. I was asked to speak in particular about fundraising based on my experience at Rice University and Columbia University. I addressed that specific request by placing it in a broader institutional context.

After briefly describing the challenges, I will then offer my sense as to how we can best respond. In doing so, I will draw in particular on my own experience at Rice University in Texas and Columbia University in New York. I would like to stress that my references to Rice and Columbia are not intended to provide a pattern to be copied. Instead, I am commenting about two universities that I know well as a way of illustrating general considerations that must be taken into account in developing strategic responses appropriate to each particular institution.

## The First Challenge:
## The Number and Quality of Students

I doubt that I have to mount an argument as to the challenge posed by student demographics in Japan, but even if only to state the obvious explicitly so that we can all focus on it, I will offer an overview of the data.

Decades of slowing birthrates have resulted in a steep decline in the numbers of young people of university age. In 1992 the number of eighteen-year-old citizens of Japan was a little over two million (2.05 million to be a little more precise). In 2012 that number was fewer than 1.2 million (or more accurately, 1.18 million). That is a decrease of more than 40 percent (42.4 percent, to be exact) in twenty years. There was in fact a slight increase in the birthrate in 2012. But the growth was small and is likely to be short-lived, with the result that the long-term trend of population decline will continue.

Over that same period, thousands of new academic departments, faculties, and even entire universities have been introduced. Many new initiatives—in particular, new undergraduate majors and graduate programs—were no doubt launched to appeal to a shrinking pool of prospective students. Whatever the motivations, there is no doubt that the total capacity of Japanese colleges and universities increased significantly.

The result is a basic mismatch between the number of students available and the number of places that colleges and universities need to fill to be financially viable. The institutions at the top of the academic hierarchy can face this challenge with relative equanimity: there are still many more applicants than spaces in those outstanding universities. But the challenge is much more pressing for hundreds of other colleges and universities. According to the most recent data, over 40 percent of private colleges and universities have empty places. The result is that almost 40 percent of private higher education institutions in Japan are facing budgetary deficits, caused in significant part by the challenges that student demographics pose.

In contrast to Japanese colleges and universities, American higher education does not (yet) face a challenge of shrinking numbers of candidates for admission. But American as well as Japanese colleges and universities face the daunting task of enlisting sufficient numbers of qualified students. Even though we in the United States are not yet confronting a shortfall in the number of young people of college or university age, we do suffer from inadequacies in our primary and secondary systems of education.

As with Japanese higher education, the challenge does not immediately confront the most elite institutions. Indeed, those colleges and universities have a higher selectivity rate than ever; that is, the percentage of applicants offered admission is lower than it has ever been. But this flourishing at the top of the hierarchy should not obscure the systemic challenge for higher education overall. It is worth underscoring this parallel between Japanese and American higher education, if only to focus all of our attention on the enormous tasks that confront the less privileged institutions in both countries.

The best of American secondary education prepares outstanding students even by international standards. Magnet schools with special admissions criteria in the public education systems across the country and elite private schools with highly qualified teachers, low student to faculty ratios, and carefully selected students (many from outside the United States), illustrate this higher quality. But the vast majority of American primary and secondary students are not educated in this small subset of schools.

Instead, most American primary and secondary students attend schools that are severely deficient by international standards. In my view, the most fundamental cause is the deprofessionalization of teaching in the United States. In contrast to systems such as those Norway or Singapore—or Japan—primary and secondary school teachers in America are not drawn from the top of the classes of college and university graduates. Instead, teachers come disproportionately from the bottom half of their graduating classes; as a result, American teachers too often and not inaccurately do not consider themselves to be the peers of other professionals in medicine, law, or even public service and higher education. This lack of self-esteem and public recognition is accentuated by the radical decentralization of American primary and secondary education, which causes the quality of schools to vary considerably from state to state and even from community to community, depending on local support.

The unionization of teachers in many public school systems may well contribute to this deprofessionalization of primary and secondary education. But as with most correlations, it is hard to determine cause and effect. Similarly, the opening of other professions to women over recent decades has resulted in an enormous loss for American education; whereas fifty years ago, a substantial fraction of the most talented young women in the United States became teachers, that fraction is much smaller today. In any case, however the effects of unionization and women's liberation are factored into the equation, the role of teaching in American primary and secondary schools has declined in status in the past three or four decades.

Perhaps the most perverse response to this challenging situation is to shift from trusting and respecting teachers to focusing more and more on testing. (In view of the central role that examinations play in the educational system in Japan, the impact of testing is a topic worthy of further comparative investigation.) In many cases at least in the American context, the increasing emphasis on periodic testing has the effect of advancing the deprofessionalization of teaching. Instead of focusing attention on the need to attract higher quality teachers, the preoccupation with testing in practice presses educators into the role of technicians who teach to the test and in the end prepare students who are less than adequately qualified for higher education that meets the most demanding international standards.

I hope that this brief overview of the inadequacies of primary and secondary education in the United States can serve to depict the way that American and Japanese colleges and universities face different but analogous challenges in enlisting adequate numbers of high quality students. To repeat, this challenge is very much attenuated for the best institutions. But for the hundreds of Japanese and the thousands of American colleges and universities that are not at the top of the hierarchy, the challenge of attracting a sufficient number of highly qualified domestic students is serious indeed.

## The Second Challenge:
## The Sources and Scale of Funding

The second challenge facing our educational systems is the sources and scale of our funding. On this challenge, both American and Japanese colleges and universities face unfavorable trend lines, particularly in regard to government support. While this financial pressure from eroding government funding has been significant in recent years in Japan, it is even more pronounced as a long-term trend in the United States.

The erosion of government funding is especially noteworthy in the best public universities in the United States. Here are two examples. At the University of Michigan, appropriations from the state of Michigan as a fraction of total revenue have steadily declined for several decades. In 2011 it stood at 6 percent of the total. At the Berkeley campus of the University of California, appropriations from the state of California accounted for 10.5 percent of the total revenue—down over 50 percent since 2003. These public universities are still extraordinary institutions for both research and education. Furthermore, in addition to state appropriations, both universities compete for and win substantial federal research grants. Yet the downward trend in the proportion of the budget funded by state appropriations is extremely problematic.

It is worth noting that even though the majority of American colleges and universities are private, about 70 percent of U.S. students are enrolled in public institutions. For much of the history of the United States, public institutions received most of their funding from their home states. These colleges and universities charged relatively low tuition and fees because most of the funding they needed came from state appropriations. This model is not unlike the model followed in most developed countries, though few countries have as many private colleges and universities. (On this point Japan, like the United States, is an exception, no doubt in significant part as a result of post-World War II pressure from America to increase the number of private institutions.)

With the downward trend in state appropriations, the tuition and fees charged to U.S. students have increased markedly. The impact has been especially significant for students who attend colleges and universities outside their home states, although charges for in-state students have also climbed considerably. In leading public universities, tuition and fees (not including food and housing) are often not much lower than at private institutions—and may be as much as $35,000 a year. Even in-state students may have to pay as much as $12,000 a year in addition to food and housing.

This shift from government support to reliance on other sources of funding has not only led to increased student charges but also to a focus by public university leaders on seeking more private donations. The so-called "flagship public universities" have especially turned more and more to fundraising from alumni/ae, other individuals and foundations, and corporations. As a result, the sources of funding for the best-known public institutions in the United States have come to resemble their private counterparts.

This shift in the sources of funding has its greatest impact on the poorest U.S. students. Insofar as local and state investments even in two-year and vocational education are in decline, opportunities for low-income students are directly reduced. Ironically, the wealthiest private colleges and universities, which commit substantial discretionary resources to need-based financial aid, may still be accessible for the most talented of students from even the lowest income groups. But even more ironically, the state institutions that have the mandate of offering upward mobility through education for all citizens cannot close the gap between rising fees and inadequate financial aid. This disempowerment of even flagship state institutions in America stands in sharp contrast to the Japanese tradition of public universities as the most elite institutions.

Yet in Japan there are also powerful downward pressures on government funding for educational institutions. The result is a tendency to seek more of the needed resources from student fees and from private sector fundraising. Consequently, there is considerable convergence in funding patterns between the two otherwise quite different systems.

### The Third Challenge: Expressing an Institutional Identity

In addressing such challenges as attracting students and grappling with resource constraints, each college or university needs to express a compelling institutional identity. Unless the institution is undergoing a total collapse and therefore requires a complete makeover, its identity will fundamentally be based on its history, which in turn will shape its future prospects. A compelling expression of this core identity will be indispensable in addressing all of the other issues that every institution confronts.

What is crucial in formulating the identity of an institution is that it express the aspiration to be more itself rather than to imitate some other institution. The temptation to try to make one institution become a copy of another one must be resisted. This temptation is especially strong when a new leader arrives from another institution and uncritically, almost unconsciously, seeks to replicate the patterns he or she knows well from the previous institution. This trap is all the more alluring when the transition is from a more junior role in a highly prestigious institution to a senior position in a less well-regarded one.

While I realize that this third challenge probably seems more abstract than the need for a sufficient number of highly qualified students and adequate resources to finance the institution, I am convinced that meeting the challenge of expressing a compelling institutional identity is in fact indispensable to addressing the other challenges that colleges and universities confront. As I turn from the challenges we face to proposing strategic responses, I will therefore begin with the third challenge and show how responding vigorously to this challenge can provide the platform for addressing the other two. To buttress—or at least to illustrate—this contention, I will refer to examples from my own experience, namely Rice University and Columbia University.

## Rice University as an Illustration

Prior to my appointment as president of Rice University, I was the dean of the Harvard Divinity School. Rice had never had a president in its history who was not a mathematician or a natural scientist. The Rice board of governors appointed a search committee to find a successor to Norman Hackerman, a very distinguished chemist who was a member of the Natural Academy of Sciences (among many other honors) and who had been president of Rice for fifteen years. Both the board and the search committee declared that the university was open to considering candidates from fields outside of science, mathematics, and engineering. But I am quite sure that this openness to historians, political scientists, or others in the humanities and social sciences did not prepare the multiple Rice constituencies for a president whose previous position was the dean of a divinity school. As the then-president of Harvard, Derek Bok, said to the search committee when asked about me, "We thought we had hidden him pretty well over there in the Divinity School." Unsurprisingly, my academic field was a prominent feature in media coverage of my appointment.

In the months between my initial discussions with the Rice search committee and my arrival as the new president, I immersed myself in the history of Rice and the current issues confronting the university. I was especially attracted to the vision of Edgar Odell Lovett, the founding president, who led the institution for almost forty years (1908–1946). Lovett was a mathematician, and he appreciated the focus on technical training that the word "institute" in the original name of Rice conveyed. But he also insisted from the beginning that Rice should be an institute of "liberal as well as technical learning." As a result of his and many other efforts, when I arrived at Rice in 1985, the university was distinctive—and, although I almost always avoid the word, we could in this instance say "unique"— among first-rate American colleges and universities in having just about equal numbers of students and faculty on the two sides of the so-called "two cultures" divide: mathematics, the natural sciences, and engineering on one side and arts, humanities, and social sciences on the other.

Along with this remarkable balance among student majors and faculty expertise, Rice had and continues to have a further impressive distinction among research universities. In the United States, there are a few other small research institutions. The California Institute of Technology is a very prestigious case in point. But because Caltech is focused almost exclusively on science and engineering, it can achieve a critical mass in particular clusters of expertise. In contrast, Rice has aspired to be a comprehensive research university while retaining the small scale of a liberal arts college.

When I arrived at Rice I was determined to make the most of the energy eager to move ahead across the institution—among members of the board of governors, the faculty, the students, and the alumni/ae. There was a palpable sense of urgency for forward movement after a prolonged period of stasis. But I also was acutely aware that we needed to preserve the highly prized core values at the heart of the institution from its earliest years.

Fortunately, there were several early vacancies in the senior administration that allowed me to recruit colleagues in leading this effort. The first was a new provost, Neal Lane. He had been a long-term faculty member, a physicist with deep roots at Rice who had left only a few years earlier in part out of frustration with the lack of forward movement at the university. He was much beloved, and his departure had been mourned even though everyone recognized that he had moved on to a leadership position as chancellor of a University of Colorado campus. His decision to return as provost was a significant marker for the advances ahead. A second early vacancy was in Rice's Wiess School of Natural Sciences. For that position we were successful in recruiting Jim Kinsey, previously chair of the Chemistry Department at the Massachusetts Institute of Technology, who was a Rice alumnus and felt energized by the prospect of returning to his alma mater and home state to make a great university even better. A third early vacancy was for the dean of engineering, where we recruited a wonderfully cultured and wide-ranging faculty member from the University of California-Berkeley, Michael Carroll. A fourth recruiting opportunity came when we determined to enhance the Shepherd School of Music by building a new faculty and sharply raising its profile; for the position of dean we attracted Michael Hammond, a gifted and charismatic leader who was then chancellor of the State University of New York (SUNY) at Purchase. Finally, we recruited a new vice president for finance and administration when the incumbent decided to retire. Against my usual instincts, this new colleague, Dean Currie, was from Harvard—from the Harvard Business School, where he was associate dean. I had not known Dean at Harvard. But he was a Texas native and immediately saw the potential for significant progress for what was already a great (though too little known) institution.

Even before I arrived at Rice, I knew it would be challenging to maintain the small scale of the institution (2,600 undergraduate students, a thousand graduate students, and 400 faculty members) and still be a major player in research and scholarship. As a reality check, I ascertained the number of faculty in the biological sciences at the University of California, Berkeley (as an example of a comprehensive research university). The number was over four hundred, or about the size of the total Rice faculty. To achieve the critical mass required for participation in substantial federally funded research in the sciences and engineering, we would therefore have to develop multidisciplinary centers of strength that could effectively compete precisely because our small scale allowed—and at least potentially encouraged—multidisciplinary research.

Happily, there was a prototype for this kind of center at the university: the Rice Quantum Institute, which enlisted faculty members and graduate students from physics, chemistry, and electrical engineering in basic research. The challenge was to develop other such centers or institutes so that every faculty member and his or her students would have a setting for multidisciplinary teaching, research, and scholarship. In practice, especially in the arts and humanities, individual writing and solo projects were of course not precluded. But in principle, all members of the Rice community would have a place to work in collaboration with colleagues.

Over a two-year period we worked closely with faculty to conceive and organize five such multidisciplinary centers. We were successful in significant part because we recruited the very best Rice faculty to take the lead, including the director of the Rice Quantum Institute, Richard Smalley, who ten years later was awarded the Nobel Prize for Chemistry for his groundbreaking research in nanotechnology during this period. The multidisciplinary centers in the sciences and engineering and also in the humanities and social sciences were instrumental in greatly increasing (in fact, more than doubling) grants for research and scholarship both from the federal government (including especially the Natural Science Foundation) and also from private foundations and corporations.

Along with focusing attention on the distinctiveness of Rice as a significant center of research and scholarship not only in spite of but at least in part because of its small scale, we also moved systematically to make the most of our core identity as an institute for liberal as well as technical learning, with student majors more or less evenly divided between mathematics, the natural sciences, and engineering on the one hand, and the arts, humanities, and the social sciences on the other. Soon after my arrival we began the process of revising the undergraduate curriculum. Based on extensive faculty deliberation, we decided to implement changes, including the development of new courses, that would enable and require all students to attain a solid grounding on both sides of the two cultures divide. Unlike many of our peer institutions in the sciences and engineering, Rice would not have only a scattering of courses in the humanities and social sciences but rather would require a coherent minor in those disciplines. Similarly, the half of the student body that majored in the arts, humanities, and social sciences would be required to complete a coherent minor in the disciplines of mathematics, the natural sciences, and engineering.

## Columbia University as a Further Illustration

As I had been at Rice, I was an outsider when I arrived at Columbia University to become its president. No other president except Dwight Eisenhower came into office with no prior Columbia affiliation—not an alumnus, not a faculty member, not an administrative role. Perhaps in part because of some sensitivity in this score, Columbia awarded me an honorary doctoral degree at the commencement before my appointment as president began. That way at least I would be able to wear Columbia academic regalia as I presided at future commencements!

Unlike Rice, which was to many a well-kept secret, Columbia has a high profile both nationally and internationally. It had been through some tough years and when I arrived had a substantial structural deficit, but the university had enormous assets and great resilience. As with Rice, the challenge was to return to its roots and make it more itself as it moved toward renewed flourishing.

As at Rice, I focused on shaping a team to lead that effort. In this case the members of the team were not plucked from across the country. Instead they were either long-term Columbians or deeply engaged and experienced New Yorkers who came from the city's government or other leading institutions. Provost Jonathan Cole exemplified the first pattern: he had left Columbia for only a few years since arriving as a freshman. Also illustrating this first pattern were Richard Naum, the vice president for development, and Anne McSweeney, the deputy vice president and special advisor to the president for development. Instances of the second pattern were the vice presidents for finance and administration: John Masten, who was the chief financial officer at the New York Public Library, and Emily Lloyd, whom we recruited from her position as New York City Commissioner of Sanitation and Environmental Protection. The exception to the rule was Alan Stone, whom we recruited from his duties at the White House in Washington, D.C. to be the public policy and advocacy vice president.

Probably Columbia's greatest asset is its location in New York City. Indeed, its full name is Columbia University in the City of New York. Yet this asset was too often not a focus of the attention of various university constituencies. In part because of its location in northern Manhattan, in Morningside Heights and Washington Heights and adjacent to Harlem, Columbia at times seemed almost apologetic about its location—even in its own literature. Descriptions would mention how it was in fact quite safe and how the resources of Midtown and Downtown Manhattan were actually readily accessible. It was of course the case that the decades of the 1970s and 1980s were difficult for New York City as a whole and northern Manhattan in particular. That recent history frequently led to a lack of full conviction as to the tremendous vitality that New York City offered.

So from the beginning of my presidency I embraced our location in New York City as a central feature of our institutional identity. We were indeed Columbia University in the City of New York. All of our literature and public announcements would trumpet this distinction from all of our peers that could not claim our home city. There would no doubt be prospective students and faculty who would find our location in northern Manhattan to be intimidating to the point that they would choose not to join us. So be it. We did not need to appeal to every prospective student or faculty member in Iowa, Arizona, or Oregon. We had to be compelling only to the most able and creative students in the small numbers we could accommodate—and there are overwhelming numbers of those most able and creative prospective colleagues all over the country and the world for whom New York City is a great attraction.

In focusing on the enormous resources of New York City, my colleagues and I recognized that we had to attend to the frayed relations that the university often had with its closest neighbors: Morningside Heights, Washington Heights, and Harlem. I made it a personal priority to become acquainted with local community and political leaders and to work with them toward aligning the interests of the university with the concerns of our neighbors. I will not pretend that Columbia always succeeded in implementing these good intentions, but I do know that many of my fondest memories of my time at Columbia are meetings with our neighbors—including discussions with community boards and elected officials during the last years of my time at Columbia when we and our neighbors were all in agreement that an expansion of the university into a portion of southern Harlem now often referred to as Manhattanville would be a win-win accomplishment for the university and for the community.

Along with its location in New York City—and in significant part as a result—Columbia has the asset of its standing as a global institution. It works both ways. Because New York is indisputably a world city, its identification with Columbia certainly raises the university's global profile. But the centuries-long development of linguistic, regional, curricular, and research resources at Columbia also strengthens the standing of New York as a world city.

These academic strengths may pale in comparison with such institutions as Wall Street and the United Nations. But the investment in language, literature, history, economics, and politics is nonetheless a core strength of Columbia and one that is critically important to New York City. This strength is one that we continue to nurture—for example, in investing in the School of International and Public Affairs (SIPA), in forging closer relations with the United Nations, and in establishing the Columbia Earth Institute under the leadership of Jeffrey Sachs.

While my colleagues and I stressed the fact that Columbia was distinguished as a university in New York City with a long-established reputation for its global profile, we also focused—at my insistence—on how central is its education for undergraduates. When I immersed myself in Columbia traditions before I arrived as president, I noted an odd set of at least apparently contradictory observations. On the one hand, Columbia projected itself outward as a university with distinguished graduate programs in the arts and sciences and excellent professional schools that all but overshadowed the education it offered undergraduates. On the other hand, I was enormously impressed with the undergraduate education it did offer, including in particular the core curriculum that was required of all students in Columbia College.

Rather than to continue to allow Columbia's undergraduate education to be lost in the midst of high-profile graduate and professional studies, we insisted that the college (and the undergraduate schools of engineering and general studies) were at the heart of the university. We called attention to the fact that all students were required to be grounded across the arts and sciences in a rigorous set of requirements refined and strengthened since its introduction in 1919. We also announced the intention to invest substantial resources in undergraduate life—a new student center; new residential facilities and improvements in existing ones; enhanced athletic, laboratory, and library facilities; and more aggressive student recruitment and financial aid.

## The Lesson to Be Learned from the Cases of Rice and Columbia

Affirming the central dimensions of Columbia's identity—our location in New York City, our long history as an international university, and our exemplary undergraduate education—was crucial for the major advances we achieved in both attracting students and raising resources. So too was celebrating the distinctive features of Rice. In both cases, embracing our core identity was crucial for other advances.

The focus on undergraduate education was not only a gesture of respect for Columbia's heritage but also a recognition of why the university had not consistently achieved the reputational ratings that its quality merited. For better or for worse, the average American who is not directly involved in higher education establishes his or her hierarchy of academic institutions based on how difficult it is to gain admission to its undergraduate unit. Insofar as Columbia did not focus on undergraduate education or even seemed to apologize for its location, applications for admission to its undergraduate schools were not as robust as should have been the case if quality alone ruled. By focusing on undergraduate education, we reversed that trend. During my time as president, applications for undergraduate admissions more than doubled. At the same time, the proportion of applicants who are admitted declined by two-thirds because a larger proportion of those admitted decided to attend.

Even as the competition for admission to Columbia's undergraduate programs increased, the visibility and attractiveness of the university as a whole—including its graduate and professional schools—resulted in increased applications across the entire institution. This increase was especially notable in applications from international students. Our higher profile, together with our greater emphasis on its history and identity as a global institution, allowed the university to increase its proportion of international students year after year. Today, students from outside the United States account for over 25 percent of the total enrollment at the university.

Rice also experienced a similar positive impact in the attraction of students. During my eight years at Rice, the number of applications for admission tripled, and the quality of those applicants also rose very substantially. To note one specific datum, in my last year at Rice, we received more applications from Merit Scholar finalists (an exceedingly demanding nationwide standard) than there were places available in the incoming class.

I am pleased to report that delineating and articulating a compelling identity continuous with an institution's history and ethos also was effective in addressing the need for resources. In the case of Rice, I have noted the doubling of federal and foundation funding for research and scholarship. But private donations also increased significantly as alumni/ae realized that the education they valued required support. In my view, Rice deferred major fund drives longer than would have been optimal, but it has now completed two substantial and successful campaigns. Similarly, annual private donations to Columbia increased year after year, especially from college alumni/ae, because they were deeply grateful for the university's recognition of their alma mater's historical identity and central role at the university. Donations set a new record in each of my nine years as president, more than tripling over those years—from $115 million to $360 million. During that period we also completed an endowment campaign, with an original goal of $1 billion that was increased to $2 billion and then finally closed at $2.84 billion—the largest campaign total achieved by any university until that time, though one that has been exceeded a few times (including most recently at Columbia itself) in the intervening decade.

To repeat in summary form the central lesson that my experience at Rice and Columbia seems to me to teach: a clear articulation of the core identity of an institution is critically important for attracting the high-quality students and the scale of funding required for vigorous forward movement.

## Implications for Other—Japanese and American—Institutions

While I am acutely aware that successes at Rice and Columbia do not by any stretch of the imagination definitively address the systemic challenges of attracting adequately prepared students in sufficient numbers and generating sufficient financial resources, I will conclude by sketching a few tentative approaches for engaging these larger issues in the Japanese as well as the American setting.

In the case of the United States, I have already stated at least by implication that the systemic solution for inadequacies in primary and secondary education is the re-professionalization of teaching as a career. I readily concede that this approach will pay off only in the long term. But I do not think that any of the other measures under discussion or in initial phases of implementation will suffice unless and until primary and secondary schools again attract a critical mass of the best and brightest college and university graduates as teachers. Teacher-training programs can and should be improved. Nationwide certifications for teachers, national standards for student attainment, more hours in classrooms by lengthening both the school day and the academic year, incentive grants for innovative ways to achieve excellence, and many other initiatives can and should be pursued. But the most critical challenge is to attract outstanding teachers and entrust the education of students to their professional judgment rather than have outsiders who are not teachers themselves micromanage the educational process.

Almost as important as attracting outstanding professionals to teaching is securing funding designed to provide adequate educational resources for all students. Current American mechanisms for funding education at all levels offer many opportunities to the sons and daughters of the wealthy that are not available to the poor or even to many in the middle class. Those opportunities begin with intellectual stimulation at home from an early age and also in a variety of preschool programs. This early advantage is compounded because so much of the funding for primary and secondary education comes from local communities and is almost always raised through property taxes. Here again, the decentralized organization of schooling in the United States stands in marked contrast to patterns in Japan. Resources available to schools form state and local sources vary widely, as do funds donated from such private support associations as completely community-based volunteer parent-teacher organizations.

The advantages are, of course, augmented further in the case of those students from well-to-do families who opt out of the public school system entirely to attend private schools. This alternative is also available to a very small number of students from low-income families who receive scholarships. In the past, religious-based schools—in particular those established by the Roman Catholic Church, which were often located in inner-city neighborhoods—also provided opportunities, but funding pressures are leading to the closing of these private schools in the poorest communities.

The challenge of adequately educating primary and secondary students and of providing the financial resources required for the entire system of higher education in the United States will in the end require substantially increased funding from government at all levels. The alternative is an ever-widening gap between the educational opportunities of the rich in comparison with the rest of society. Avoiding this outcome will require strategic responses from communities across the United States, from neighborhood civic and school support organizations to advocacy organizations at all levels, and from local, state, and federal governments.

You will not be surprised to hear that I have no solution to offer to the underlying demographic problem that Japanese colleges and universities face. But the approach that I propose exploring is to combine the challenge of shrinking student numbers with the broader challenge of funding to enhance the quality of the Japanese higher education overall. While the inadequacies in the funding streams for Japanese higher education demand attention in their own right, this challenge is not unrelated to the demographic trend in student numbers.

One very direct way to address the challenge of declining numbers of eighteen year olds is to downsize the capacity of colleges and universities. The most dramatic version of this option would be simply to accept, even facilitate, the closing of a significant number of colleges and universities. A less dramatic alternative would be to reduce the numbers of students at a college or university, with the prospect of increasing the quality of education for those smaller numbers of students. But this alternative is available only if colleges and universities have substantial—and increasing—sources of funding in addition to existing tuition and fees. Insofar as government policy increases dependence on tuition and fees, reducing the number of students is simply not an option. Put positively, the policy implication of any option that reduces the number of students at a college or university is that other sources of support—government funding, private fundraising, income from intellectual property—increase so that the institution is less dependent on tuition and fees from students.

One further approach to the combined challenges of student numbers and overall funding pressures is to explore aggressive prospects for substantially increasing the enrollment of international students. I know that the higher education community in Japan, prodded in part by the government, has for some years been exploring how to increase international exchanges. Indeed, there is an impressive tradition of government support for such exchanges. In my own family, our daughter Katherine had the honor of receiving a Monbusho Scholarship some twenty years ago. It enabled her to study with fellow students and researchers from China and South Korea—in the one language they all had in common: Japanese. It is at least conceivable that such far-sighted initiatives could be expanded to see how feasible it is for Japan to become a regional center for higher education and research, a goal that would at the same time contribute to the development of an inclusive community of nations in the Asia-Pacific region.

A significant increase in international enrollments is certainly not beyond imagining, as the comparative data show. Germany attracts about 250,000 international students, and China hosts over 300,000. There is no reason that Japan, which currently hosts fewer than 140,000 international students, cannot aspire to similar numbers. The United States hosts the largest number of international students (at 765,000). But international students represent under 4 percent of total U.S. enrollments. Compare that to France and Germany (at around 12 percent of total enrollments) or even more dramatically to the United Kingdom (at over 18 percent). Still more remarkable is Asia-Pacific neighbor Australia (at over 21 percent). There is, in short, room for a major expansion of the international student population in Japanese colleges and universities.

At its most expansive, this approach would develop campuses and curricula attractive to substantial numbers of students from across the Asia-Pacific region. It would build on the fact that China, South Korea, and Taiwan are the largest current international suppliers of students to Japan. No doubt, existing smaller exchange partnerships with the United States and with Germany among other European countries would continue. But the new feature would be an effort to scale up a significantly larger presence of international students with the appeal that such interaction would be cultivated to allow cooperation across the Asia-Pacific region, as our daughter Katherine experienced two decades ago.

This initiative would raise a host of questions. Should instruction be available in Chinese and English as well as Japanese? Should an effort be included to recruit students from India? In spite of the historical tensions, might Japan be able to develop as a center, as more or less neutral ground, where students from China, Taiwan, South Korea, Malaysia, India, Myanmar, Australia, Vietnam, the United States, and Japan lived and studied together for at least brief periods—perhaps a semester at a time? All of these questions and many more are already under exploration through the Global 30 Project for Establishing Core Universities for Internationalization and within its thirteen selected universities, with special focus at such institutions as Ritsumeikan Asia-Pacific University. It is easy to be cynical about such initiatives, especially since colleges and universities are often capable of fierce resistance to change. Yet it is crucial to encourage and support all such programs, not only to generate needed resources but also because they represent efforts to fashion the building blocks for inclusive communities.

Higher education in both Japan and the United States faces a major challenge in attracting sufficient numbers of adequately prepared students and in generating the resources required to execute this responsibility. But as daunting as is the challenge, it is also an opportunity to provide leadership in developing communities of future colleagues—communities that are inclusive across socio-economic strata and also across national and cultural divisions. This leadership is urgently needed now more than ever and will certainly continue to be required for the foreseeable future.

# 5    What Is the Good Life?

IN MY INTRODUCTION I noted that framing issues for the next generation may help to focus our attention on the challenges we currently face. In this chapter and the next, I will give a further testing of that premise. To begin, in examining the question of "What is the good life?" I will seek to summarize how education contributes to the global quest for inclusive communities.

Because we live in twenty-first century America, we pretty much automatically begin reflection on the good life with a focus on the individual. We ask what will result in an individual's sense of accomplishment or happiness. To use the shorthand summary often attributed to Sigmund Freud, we refer to the need to pursue satisfaction in love and work. But this focus remains on the individual. While we acknowledge that relationships almost certainly play a role—perhaps even a crucial or central one—in that sense of accomplishment, satisfaction, or happiness, we start with the individual persons who in turn may be related to each other.

This almost-automatic starting point for our thinking about the good life results in significant part from our history. While contemporary experience is certainly the product of many traditions, for most of us the dominant patterns derive from Western individualism, in particular those patterns that have developed in the last few centuries. Yet precisely because this starting point seems almost self-evident, we should subject it to searching examination and compare it carefully to other traditions,

---

This chapter is based on a talk given at the University of Florida to an orientation session for all incoming students in October 2012. A version of the second half of the chapter also served as the core of my commencement address for Pace University at Madison Square Garden, New York, in May 2014.

including long stretches in Western history in which the community is construed as primary.

In the first half of this chapter I will conduct that examination. I apologize in advance that, in order to identify the general issues that cut across particular personal, social, and cultural traditions, this diagnostic exercise will be quite abstract. Based on this examination or diagnosis, I will then sketch the prescription that seems to be called for by offering three bits of advice for us as we seek to live the good life.

## Western Individualism and Traditional Communities

The various forms of individualism that have risen in the West are of course themselves social and cultural products of quite particular traditions. Such traditions may well aspire to be universally relevant or even universally compelling, yet they are nonetheless rooted in specific spatial and temporal communities. A self-aware individualism must therefore acknowledge that its identity has been shaped by particular histories and communities and not simply assume that all individuals everywhere can be abstracted from their traditions and be expected to react in predictable ways that take no account of social and cultural differences.

This imperative is especially urgent in the cases of traditional communities that view themselves as under assault from Western culture. These communities have their own patterns of authority, which typically depend on personal relationships established over generations. Members of such communities do not regard the forces they resist as culturally neutral but rather as ideologically antagonistic. From their perspective, this individualistic alternative is embedded in its own set of historical patterns.

The resistance of traditional communities to Western individualism is not only conceptual but also institutional. Though the West acknowledges the formative influence of personal relations, especially within the private space of the immediate family, it also focuses attention on relatively impersonal structures to enhance individual well-being: market mechanisms, bureaucracies, and media. In contrast, traditional communities look to many other public and well-established arrangements of personal interaction: extended families, informal alliances, small-scale cooperatives, village elders, and religious authorities.

The Western style of connecting the individual to the larger society directly through markets, bureaucracies, or media too often ignores or circumvents the network of intermediate institutions that animates traditional communities. Institutional patterns taken for granted in the modern West effectively call into question the authority and viability of traditional relationships. Here is a brief sampling of instances: large-scale markets may disrupt personal exchanges; broadly based elections may undermine hereditary authority; women who earn money through small businesses may upset established gender roles. Not surprisingly, this undermining of long-established practices elicits resistance in traditional societies. The beneficiaries of these established patterns as well as the other members of the community refuse to relinquish the rich network of highly personal relationships that provides order and texture to their daily lives.

While communities are defined by boundaries of all kinds, impersonal mechanisms can in principle connect all individuals to each other across divides of background, location, or family identity. The challenge that the processes of globalization pose for communities everywhere is to nurture particular traditions and intimate relationships while at the same time affirming an inclusiveness that is open to all. This endeavor can be construed as an attempt to connect individuals universally to each other. But it can also be envisioned as an effort to incorporate particular communities into increasingly more inclusive ones, a process that preserves valued historical patterns even as it encourages openness to the affirmations of other traditions.

## Testimony from Religious Traditions

Central to the deeply personal, social, and cultural grounding of many—perhaps all—traditional communities are religious faith and practice. In their beliefs, rituals, and ethical imperatives, members of such communities affirm their identity, which gives adherents a sense of distinction from other traditions. Religious affirmation therefore often reinforces the boundaries that separate particular communities from each other.

Yet religious traditions additionally provide substantial resources for meeting the challenge of incorporating individuals not only into their immediate communities but also into larger, more inclusive ones. Certainly some appropriations of religious traditions appear highly individualistic, espousing direct connections between the individual person and the ultimate or the divine. But across traditions there are also strong affirmations of the communal basis for any such individual identity, a basis that frequently deploys religious beliefs and practices to point beyond every local or particular community and connect to larger human, natural, and even divine realities.

Chinese and Jewish traditions have perhaps been the most direct in focusing on human connection as the way to final truth, even if they do not consistently press toward increasingly inclusive communities. For the Confucian, there is no access to the ultimate except through social relationships. Similarly, though there are certainly significant and arresting exceptions, the dominant pattern of Jewish commitment has been to stress the communal character of relationship to the divine.

Hindu traditions offer a striking illustration of powerful individualism dependent on particular communities even as it aspires to universal inclusion. The vast diversity of Hindu traditions includes the central affirmation that *atman* is *brahman*, that the self is one with the ultimate. This affirmation is crucial not only in the history of Indian philosophy but also for modern Indian humanism. It is, in a sense, highly individualistic. Yet despite this identification of the self with the ultimate, Indian traditions build on community solidarity as the foundation for any individual attainment and also construe the ultimate as all-inclusive.

The Hindu heresy of Buddhism exhibits the same pattern in its myriad forms. The earliest Buddhist traditions flatly deny that there is a self at all: the Hindu affirmation of *atman* is negated and becomes the insistence on *anātman*, not self. In later developments, this insistence becomes an acceptance of *śūnyatā*, the emptiness of all reality. Yet in and through their remarkable spectrum of critical appropriations of Hindu traditions, Buddhists embrace the communities through which individuals advance, beginning with the *sangha*, the order of monks that became the bearer of Buddhist traditions.

Across the range of Christian churches there is a similar pattern: Roman Catholics may be intentionally corporate, Orthodox Christians may nurture a sense of connection to the cosmos as a whole, and Protestants may focus on the individual self. Yet all Christians affirm the crucial role of faithful communities in mediating the relationship of the human to the divine, which for many Christians is also a community.

Islam offers a final example, one especially apt since so much of the most forceful resistance to Western individualism is anchored in Muslim conviction. Like other religious traditions, Islam incorporates enormous diversity—and is often quite public in its internal disagreements. As in other religious communities there are mystics who claim direct communion with the ultimate, with Allah. But for virtually all Muslims, the role of the community is indispensable to the faithful life. In repudiating Western social and cultural patterns, advocates of Islam are rejecting what they deem to be a corrosive individualism that undermines this indispensable role of the community.

## The Challenge for a Conflicted World

In contrast to this testimony from religious traditions, the consumer society and mass culture of the West at least appear to extract the individual from particular communities. As the Internet expands, this Western individualism takes on new intensity. Across the Web, new definitions of personal relationships and self-promotion are flourishing.

Yet even this reductionist, Web-enabled individualism is in the end dependent on particular communities, including the new online communities that it creates. This dependence is sometimes recognized: there is much talk today of the connectivity of the net. This virtual connectivity may even be twinned with a yearning for a sense of togetherness that has been lost in offline life.

But nostalgia is not an adequate guide for the way forward. Instead, it is crucial to affirm this impulse for community while also remaining committed to the values of individualism, including civil liberties and human rights. This double affirmation entails significant ramifications. Commitment to the values of individualism requires that a community be open to outsiders yet also be prepared to see its own shortcomings. It calls for a community that allows self-criticism and, in principle, the incorporation of members from other traditions.

In practice, communities that are both self-critical and inclusive are admittedly rare. Opposition does not stem only from uncritical and exclusionist traditionalists. Instead, any affirmation of community, even if it is self-critical and inclusive, must also contend with precisely the individualism that has characterized much of Western social and cultural history, especially since the Enlightenment.

This contention between the affirmation of community and the powerful attractions of individualism is in my view the way we should frame our reflections on the good life. It is a more adequate starting point than a focus on the sense of accomplishment, satisfaction, or happiness of individuals. From within this frame, I will therefore presume to offer three bits of advice for all of us as we seek to understand, appropriate, and, we can hope, live the good life.

## Aim High

My first bit of advice is to aim high. This counsel is in significant part the direct result of the individualism that has shaped us all. It is all the more powerful because of the way it captures core motifs of our common heritage. We can and should take responsibility for our own aspirations and achievements. To live a good life therefore invites us—and in the end requires us—to aim high.

In our colleges and universities we learn much that might lead to skepticism or even to cynicism. We may still be confident that some problems have exact solutions. But we also know that many issues do not lend themselves to clear and unambiguous resolutions. That is a gain. I at least hope that one outcome of our education is what psychologists who develop tests of personality traits call "tolerance of ambiguity."

But while this tolerance of ambiguity almost unavoidably includes a healthy dose of skepticism, it need not lapse into cynicism. By all means, we should be dubious about the conventional wisdom, the taken-for-granted verities, the unquestioned assumptions of our times. In short, we should think critically. We need to compare what is generally accepted here and now with what has been different elsewhere or might one day be different here. Such constructive criticism is the opposite of cynicism. It is engaged. It searches. It cares.

This engaged, searching, and caring attitude or orientation is what I mean when I encourage us to aim high. In our studies we learn something of the discipline involved and the satisfaction attained in setting demanding goals. To aim high requires enough of a critical sense not to be totally submerged in satisfying immediate needs and wants. To aim high entails a certain reserve about the roles society ever more insistently assigns to us. To aim high is in effect to engage in a lover's quarrel with our world, a quarrel that expresses restlessness with what is on behalf of what might be.

Heights are sometimes dangerous. We climb up in the hope that the view is worth it. So in seeking to balance commitment to community with our own individual aspirations, we should aim high.

## Let Go

As a counterpart of any urging that we aim high, I offer a second bit of advice: let go. If aiming high is a testament to the vigor of individualism, letting go is a recognition of the limits of one person's pushing on all alone. The individual and his or her various communities do in fact require each other.

If we set our sights, our goals, our aspirations high, we will have to be on guard against the temptation to be so vigorously engaged, so earnestly searching, so deeply caring that we take ourselves too seriously. We should not do that. Crucial as our contribution is, everything does not depend on us. We should love and work vigorously, give it our best shot, but then let go. We need to keep the kind of comic distance that comes from seeing ourselves in perspective.

Comic distance and the sense of humor that comes with it are virtues in their own right. Keeping a sense of perspective also allows us to appreciate the vantage point of others, to listen carefully, and to find common ground that allows shared forward movement. This capacity is crucial for responding to adversity, which of course will confront all of us at more than one point in our lives whether we live the good life or not.

To be intensely involved brings its own satisfaction. But to be only and always fully engaged also takes its toll. We all need occasions to experience the delights of relaxation, play, and celebration of all sorts. The counterpoint to the satisfaction of involvement is the pleasure of letting go. This letting go is an expression of, and also expresses, joy and gratitude: delight and thankfulness not only in the contributions we are able to make but also in the accomplishments of others even when our own fall short. Only if we let go of exclusive preoccupation with our own concerns and projects do we experience this sense of joy and gratitude. So along with our caring, our searching, our engagement, we need to allow ourselves to let go.

## Keep Moving

My final bit of advice as we seek to live a good life that balances the strengths of individualism with the values of community is to keep moving.

If we let go of exclusive preoccupation with our own concerns and projects, we are already on the way. But we should keep moving. Comic distance alone is not enough. To integrate the satisfaction of involvement with the joy and gratitude of letting go requires commitment to a cause that we find compelling.

I do not know what that cause may be for each of us. But I hope that all of us will over time find communities that elicit our enthusiastic participation. Through trust in and commitment to such communities we will be able to collaborate with others in causes that enrich, to use Freud's formulation again, our own love and work.

This kind of collaboration is crucial for keeping our larger society vital, nourishing, and fruitful. But to keep moving in this way is a struggle. We can easily become so engrossed in our own concerns and projects that we are no longer genuinely open to larger issues and causes and communities. Then we dry up, we stagnate, we die the slow death of being wrapped up only in ourselves.

I am aware that this contrast between the death of being wrapped up only in ourselves and the life that breaks out of this prison and keeps moving may seem quite abstract. In an attempt to make the point more concrete, more down-to-earth, I invite you to an excursion in geography for an illustration that impressed itself vividly on me during a trip to what we in the West call the Middle East.

## The Dead Sea vs. the Sea of Galilee

If we look at a map of the area that comprises Jordan, Israel, and the region variously characterized as Judea and Samaria, the occupied Palestinian territories, or the West Bank and Gaza, we notice immediately that there are two sizeable bodies of water in it: a large almost rectangular one in the south and a smaller pear- or teardrop-shaped one in the north. The two bodies of water are, respectively, the Dead Sea and the Sea of Galilee. They are connected by the River Jordan, which runs pretty much north to south.

The Sea of Galilee is at the heart of a vital area in which both farming and fishing flourish because of the fresh water available to nourish such enterprises. In fact, water from the Sea of Galilee sustains much of Israel. Water is pumped to holding towers on nearby hills about a hundred yards higher than the lake itself. From that slight elevation, the water flows through a system of aqueducts stretching all over the country, spreading the vitality of the Sea of Galilee far and wide.

In contrast to the vitality of the Sea of Galilee, the Dead Sea is . . . dead. The Dead Sea has also at times been called the Salt Sea, and it has the highest concentration of salt of any body of water in the world. As a result, it can sustain no life whatsoever. It is stagnant and, excepting the ports of entry into the main body of water, it is surrounded by arid desert and unrelieved desolation.

The contrast between the Sea of Galilee and the Dead Sea is, then, a stark embodiment of the contrast between fruitfulness and barrenness, between nourishment and stagnation, between life and death.

The explanation of the difference between the two bodies of water is as straightforward as the contrast is stark. The Sea of Galilee is fed by two rivers and other lesser streams at its north end; it in turn feeds the River Jordan from its southern tip. In contrast, water from the River Jordan empties into the Dead Sea but has no outlet from it except through evaporation. The Sea of Galilee both receives and gives water; the Dead Sea only takes it.

This fact of geography concretely embodies the truth that underlies my advice to keep moving. It is a truth that we all know from personal experience. If we only take, if we always watch out for number one, if we make sure we get what we want regardless of those around us, then we not only do not nourish others. We also die ourselves. In the end we squeeze out all vitality in our connections to others, and because we cannot live altogether in isolation, we have only the most stunted existence ourselves. Over against this way of death—this way so vividly represented by the Dead Sea—stands the way of life mapped out for us by the Sea of Galilee: our lives are nourishing and fruitful when we receive gratefully and in turn give to others generously.

## The Good Life

I am certainly not under the illusion that seeing this contrast renders the choice itself easy. In fact, all of us struggle every day between the sharp extremes etched on the map of our lives as the Dead Sea and the Sea of Galilee. We are all captive of our own preoccupations; thus we are ever in need of deliverance from ourselves. In the end, this liberation, this deliverance from ourselves, is a gift. As we receive this most wonderful gift, we are in turn enabled not only to get but also to give, not only to take but also to expend ourselves for others, not only to embody the dry barrenness of death but also to express the lush fruitfulness of life.

This gift of life, in all its abundance, is never ours to possess. It is always a flowing stream that we receive and pass on. The contrast between the Sea of Galilee and the Dead Sea may help us all to focus our awareness on our struggle to move beyond being wrapped up only in our own needs and wants and to embrace larger issues, causes, communities.

As all of us wrestle with the question of what is the good life, I therefore urge us to focus not only on individual happiness and accomplishment—on our love and our work—as aims in themselves but also to recognize that such goals can be attained only as we engage larger issues, participate in ever more inclusive communities, and commit ourselves to causes that in the end embrace all of humanity, indeed the whole cosmos.

The good life cannot be devoted to less than this encompassing goal of inclusive communities. To pursue the good life in this sense requires that we aim high, let go, and keep moving. I encourage all of us to devote ourselves to this lifelong pursuit.

# 6   More Words for Students

I NOTED in my introduction that I have been engaged with the issues of commitment and community for over five decades. During four of those decades I was in the position of addressing students from a leadership position. You will be relieved that I will not inflict on you the full range of those speeches. But I do think that a sampling of a very small subset of these talks might be helpful as we engage the challenges ahead. I therefore include, in a way that can easily be skipped over, three conversations with students that underscore my concern for the values and commitments of coming generations.

## Challenges of the Twenty-first Century

The challenges of this century can be construed broadly: the environment, foreign policy, finance, and global health, as those issues cut across the sectors of business, government, and civil society. While I will comment on a handful of such challenges, I will not elaborate any of them in detail. Instead I will note how they are indicative of the daunting array of issues we face, from the massively global to the intensely personal.

---

The first section of this chapter is from a talk given at Yale University in February 2010 to student leaders at the Ivy League Summit X, under the overall theme of "Fearless Leadership Through the Challenges of the Twenty-first Century." The second section is drawn from remarks as a guest commencement speaker to graduating students at Rice University in May 2008. The final selection, entitled "Lessons from Lobéké," was the core of my commencement address at Columbia University in May 1999, given two years before I joined the International Rescue Committee.

First, at the most encompassingly global end of the spectrum is the fact that we as a human community are clearly expending resources beyond the level of long-term sustainability. There may be quibbles about time frames. But virtually no responsible climate scientist would disagree with the proposition that current levels of carbon emissions will over the intermediate or long run undermine human life as we know it.

Second, we are confronted with a series of challenges raised by the marked imbalance in the allocation of resources among human beings. The most dramatic example is the contrast between the resources of the developed world and the developing world—to put it bluntly, between rich and poor countries. But also within countries, notably the United States, there are massive disparities: between the top stratum of income and wealth and everyone else; and between the resources devoted to senior citizens, which are huge, and the investments made in the very young, which are scandalously small.

A third challenge we face is that we have failed to align private incentives with public standards. We strongly and rightly encourage personal initiative and reward success based on entrepreneurial inventiveness and energy and discipline. But we are less effective in ensuring that standards of responsibility are met so that the larger public is not the victim of private aggrandizement.

Fourth, while globalization is a powerful and overall salutary force, it has the potential to undermine traditional communities. This challenge is especially difficult because there are certainly traditional patterns that can and should be called into question. The issue is whether questionable practices in local communities can be appropriately criticized without insisting that the conventional wisdom of the individualistic West is the only adequate alternative.

If the ecological question of sustainability is at the most encompassingly global end of the spectrum, the fifth challenge is at the most personal extreme, though it is still also universal. It is the challenge of our own mortality. Especially in the developed world, we are living much longer and dying more slowly and with greater agony. This challenge is not one that you are likely to face in the near future. But think of your grandparents, or even your parents. We struggle against death as if we were able to defeat it. We will need to confront this illusion and rebalance the resources we are allocating to address it. Only as we acknowledge the limits of individual self-assertion will we be able to grapple with the conflicted issues involved in our approach to death and dying.

What is crucial across this whole range of challenges is that they cannot be addressed as issues that confront us simply as individuals. "Fearless leadership" may be required to get "through" such issues. But it cannot be take-no-prisoners, winner-take-all leadership. The challenges are in fact so daunting that being a little afraid rather than completely fearless may be in order.

All five challenges represent the downside of the explosive dynamism unleashed by economic and political developments over the last four or five centuries, initially in the West and increasingly globally. That dynamism has had a very substantial upside in increased prosperity and more widespread participation in governance. But the current trends that result from this set of developments are far from completely attractive even if they were sustainable.

The unattractive features of these trends are rooted in an uncritical individualism. Paradoxically, globalization may in some respects exacerbate this individualism because, in both economic and cultural ways, it seems to relate individuals to each other without relating to any intervening institutions. There are, of course, indispensable institutional structures—at the very least, markets for economic relationships and various media, including the Internet, for cultural connections. But the invisible hand of the market and the virtual community of the Internet may have the effect of undermining the more particular communities that shape a sense of shared identity and mutual responsibility.

A utopian response to this concern about undermining particular communities would be to argue for a global community that encompasses all people and relates them to each other through global media and a global market. If and as a political system emerges that can set standards for such a global order and thereby avoid even worse imbalances in resource distribution and environmental degradation, such a utopian vision may be attractive. But in the meantime, I would urge you as leaders for the twenty-first century to focus as well on strengthening the more particular communities that shape all of us as individuals.

Many of you will exercise leadership through the major institutions that dominate the social structure of the developed world. Some of you will become successful business executives, managing partners of law firms, or political leaders. Others of you will be teachers and artists, writers and researchers, doctors and counselors. Almost all of you will also live in families and other intimate communities. You will reside in neighborhoods—whether in small towns or suburbs of larger cities or major metropolitan areas that nonetheless have many sub-communities within them.

In all of those settings, you will have opportunities to move beyond your own professional and individual preoccupations. I encourage you to do that. It may mean that you participate vigorously in a religious community or another civic association committed to a local, national, or global cause. Or it may mean that you press the powerful institutions where you are employed to take into account the communities at the margin of their economic and political calculations. Whether from a base at work or at home, you can contribute toward connecting your core responsibilities to broader communities that include in particular those too often excluded from an individualistic and market-driven order that almost unavoidably favors the already well-to-do.

## Toward Inclusive Communities

A feature of our public life in recent years has been a steady erosion of the standing of the United States in the view of friends and foes alike around the world. Global opinion polls confirm what those of us who travel abroad know from our personal experience. Whether our journeys are to Latin America or Western Europe or Asia or Africa, we hear often stridently anti-American voices. The charges range widely. Members of more traditional communities, including many in majority Muslim societies, attack what they see as our immoral hedonism and our irreligious secularism. Cosmopolitans, in contrast, are offended by what they take to be our self-righteous moralism and religiosity that lead to unilateral actions even as we abandon long-held commitments to openness, generosity, and respect for human rights.

I will not pretend to respond to this at times contradictory litany of charges. I mention it because I am convinced that becoming more aware of how others view us can help us to see ourselves more clearly. As we seek to learn from the charges leveled against us, I propose the hypothesis that underlying the allegations in all their variety is an illuminating set of questions about how we as individuals relate to the communities in which we participate.

To test this hypothesis, I invite you to picture yourself in a series of concentric circles as a way of representing your participation in increasingly inclusive communities.

You are at the center of this series—in effect, the smallest circle. There are those who concentrate almost all of their attention on this central point. In your studies you have learned about the enormous power of individualism as it has developed in the West. But you have also learned to question the brand of unbridled individualism that focuses on the self as separate from the various communities in which we participate.

So consider the first circle beyond the individual—the communities with which you identify most closely. Here is a sampling: a partner; your family; a neighborhood, village, or town that you call home; an ethnic group that you embrace as your own; a religious or secular tradition that you affirm even if you also at times quarrel with it. Such communities are crucial for defining the identity that each of us appropriates—makes our own—in the course of our lives.

But we also know that none of these particular communities stands alone. In the university, a place of increasing diversity, you have had an opportunity to learn from each other. Happily, many of you have made the most of this opportunity. We can hope that as a result you will never be able even to think of yourself as completely separate from the other communities around you.

But the temptation to think of ourselves as separate from other communities also confronts universities. When I first arrived at Rice University, there was a deeply engrained tendency to contrast life on campus with what was "beyond the hedges." In the intervening decades, Rice has become more connected to Houston and the larger world. RSVP, the Rice Student Volunteer Program, which was started during my first year here, is one illustration. Rice's cooperation with the Houston Independent School District is another example. A more recent case is the Partnership for the Advancement and Immersion of Refugees (PAIR), founded in 2006 to work with refugee children in Houston. Rice has also increasingly reached out to international partners. This pattern of relating more and more both to Houston and to global civil society hearkens back to the founders of Rice: Edgar Odell Lovett, the first president, who was in office for thirty-eight years, had affiliations to educational institutions worldwide; and Captain James A. Baker, trustee extraordinaire for fifty years, had unsurpassed connections in Houston.

Still, the lessons learned here are only the beginning of what will be a life-long need to resist the allure of separation from others. Many of you come from privileged families. All of you now have the benefit of an elite education. As a result, most of you will become—or already are—members of the most socioeconomically advantaged stratum of American and other societies.

Among the most troubling trends in this country is the increasing elective isolation of the most affluent of our citizens. In the face of inadequate investment in public goods and services, the well-to-do retreat into private clubs and behind gated communities. As you commence from the university to the opportunities of leadership ahead of you, remember one of the lessons you have learned here: we enrich our lives through our experience of multiple traditions, and we impoverish ourselves if we attempt to retreat behind the hedges.

Beyond our most immediate communities—family, home neighborhood, ethnic group, religious tradition, campus, gated community—are larger circles. A big cluster comprises our various nations. And the one that is most in danger of thinking of itself as self-subsistent, as enclosed in a circle that has the capacity to be self-contained, is the country that too often still prides itself on being the only remaining superpower.

Recent years have provided incontrovertible evidence against the proposition that any country, even if it can seem to dominate an entire continent, can be complete in itself. The United States is, in the end, connected not only to Canada and Mexico but also to Central and South America, Europe, Asia, and Africa. We are involved whether or not we have a national interest narrowly conceived. Latin America has increasingly asserted its independence in ways that certainly affect the United States. The Balkans are not only a concern of Europe. Relations across the divided Korean peninsula affect us whether or not we have an antiballistic missile system. In the long run we are not insulated from the AIDS pandemic, civil war, or famine in Africa. And whatever might have seemed plausible a decade ago, even those who routinely practice denial are now aware that we cannot unilaterally declare global warming to be an issue that can safely be allowed to heat up on the back burner.

Even if we recognize the need to move beyond our nationalisms, the circumference of the next larger concentric circle is less than sharply defined. The global reach of transportation and communication systems and the economic power of multinational corporations indicate that worldwide networks are more than simply nice ideas. At the same time, the allegiance that the supranational or even the universally human commands is still weaker than our more particular loyalties, as is evident in the very limited authority granted to institutions of international governance.

The ideal of the human race, humankind, humanity as a whole has fascinated visionaries for millennia. It is often shrouded in a mist of wishes or a fog of ideologies or the mystery of religious symbolism. But this ideal of the human as such may still provide leverage against our provincialisms.

I have spent a lot of time in countries that are struggling with the aftermath and often the continuing impact of violent conflict. Most recently, I have been in Afghanistan, Pakistan, Sudan, the Democratic Republic of Congo, Mali, Jordan, and Syria. My colleagues and I in the International Rescue Committee go to places with large numbers of people uprooted by war in order to provide emergency relief and then to work with individuals and communities to rebuild disrupted lives.

This work provides a perspective on the provincialism of our usual view of the world and challenges those of us in the United States to do closer to our fair share of the investment in agriculture, basic health care, and education (especially of girls and women) that is crucial for sustainable development worldwide. This is a set of issues in which the self-deception of Americans is staggering. Polls consistently show that most of us think we as a nation are more generous than other countries in providing economic aid to the developing world. In fact, of the twenty-two most developed economies, we rank near the bottom in the percentage of our gross national product devoted to assistance: about two-tenths of 1 percent.

To bring that dry statistic to life, think of a country's gross national product as a ten-dollar bill; of that ten dollars, the most generous nation, Norway, gives a dime for development assistance, while we contribute less than two cents. And even if we add in all nongovernmental donations—personal contributions, corporate gifts, and foundation grants—that amounts to only another two cents for a total of less than a nickel out of ten dollars. That is a disgrace, especially in view of our own past performance.

In the late 1940s, at the height of the Marshall Plan, the fraction of the U.S. federal budget committed for foreign assistance was over 18 percent—an astonishingly large proportion, which no doubt underlies our national self-perception of American generosity. By the early 1960s, this percentage had dropped from 18 percent to 3 percent. Today the figure is under 1 percent, less than one-third of the level in the early 1960s and a twenty-fold decline since 1948. To his credit, President George W. Bush at the outset of his first term pressed to increase publicly funded foreign assistance, in particular through his initiative to counter the AIDS pandemic. For a few years the commitment of the United States to humanitarian develop-ment aid increased as a percentage of our gross national product. We even rose from dead last among the twenty-two most developed countries to second to last! But with recent budget pressures, the percentage has again declined. We as a nation can surely do better than that if, in our affirmation of national citizenship, we also identify with a larger circle, a community that is not confined to a single country.

Yet even if the ideal of the human as such provides some leverage against the provincialism of tribe and nation, it also points toward still more inclu-sive communities. For too many centuries in too many traditions, we have celebrated the human as above the natural. We now know that here too our connections with the larger world are crucial—and that our ignorance of those connections threatens the viability of the Earth as an ecosystem. We must therefore move not only beyond individualism, communalism, and nationalism but also beyond humanism and even humanitarianism.

In this way, each circle points beyond itself and cannot be self-con-tained—not the individual, not our closest communities, not our nations, not humanity as a whole. This recognition shapes both our ideas and our actions. So I invite you to participate vigorously in the communities that elicit your belonging; to exercise your citizenship and provide leadership in this country and in the nations around the world that you call home; to work together for the ideal of humanity so that it may become the reality we hope for, we anticipate, and we ever so imperfectly embody. But be aware as well that in all of your activity you are part of a larger reality in which we live and move and have our being, which we may venture to trust and which calls for our allegiance. As you commence from this wonderful university, stretch your minds, your imaginations, your sensibilities toward some such larger loyalty and more encompassing commitment.

That you will apprehend, appreciate, and affirm participation in such increasingly inclusive communities is a hope I express for each one of you: may it afford you liberation from the prison of self-preoccupation.

As for all of us individually, and so also for the United States as a nation, we will gain traction in countering those who attack us out of either anger or sadness if we embrace the multiple communities in which we participate. To do so counters the charge of a self-indulgent individualism that repudiates shared values. It also eschews the self-righteous confidence or moralistic certitude that allows an easy or early recourse to unilateral action. Finally, it reaffirms core American commitments to openness, generosity, and human rights.

As you are awarded your degrees from this wonderful university, and as you participate not only in the communities closest to you but also in the increasingly inclusive communities that you will unavoidably encounter, I wish each one of you all the best for all of our sake.

## Lessons from Lobéké

As Columbia graduates, you stand in a proud tradition of alumni achievement, and you therefore also inherit the responsibilities that this privilege confers. To illuminate the special responsibilities you now assume, I propose that we gain a sense of perspective by looking from greater than usual distance. To that end, I invite you to share in a trip my wife Nancy and I took in late December 1998 and early January 1999 to visit our daughter Stephanie, who has lived for several years in Central Africa, for most of that time in a remote village named Dioula at the edge of the Lobéké Forest in southeastern Cameroon. The trip was fascinating for us as a family. But the very local context of her village also offers a provocative angle of vision for considering global issues that we all face.

As you commence from this center of learning, I therefore invite you to consider three lessons from Lobéké—lessons that bear on our lives as members of ethnic communities, as actors in the world economy, and as participants in our planetary ecosystem.

The village in which Stephanie was living comprises sixty-seven families, just under five hundred people in all, from two ethnic groups: the dominant Bangando and the Baka, a minority in this village, although better known in the West because it is one of a half-dozen groups often lumped together as "Pygmies."

Outside observers typically characterize the Bangando as "farmers" and the Baka as "hunter-gatherers." As a matter of historical fact, the Bangando have settled in villages, in rectangular stick, mud, and thatch houses, and have cultivated a variety of crops in gardens carved out of the forest. In contrast, the Baka have tended to live further into the forest, in distinctively rounded woody vine and large-leaf houses, and have sustained themselves more directly from wild plants and animals. The Bangando and the Baka also have different languages and distinct craft, music, dance, and ceremonial traditions.

The potential would appear to be great for all the predictable stereotyping and conflict between two groups. On this score, contemporary Africa is certainly not immune to the contagion that over the years has infected Northern Ireland, Sri Lanka, and Iraq, among many other countries. Consider the tension and the potential and actual violence between whites and blacks in Zimbabwe and South Africa; between Tutsi and Hutu in Rwanda; and yes, on occasion between Bangando and Baka in Cameroon.

Yet the Baka and the Bangando not only live together in a very small place; they also learn from each other. Contrary to the stereotypes, the Bangando hunt as well as farm, using techniques taught to them by their Baka neighbors, and the Baka cultivate crops to supplement their forest-based diets. Baka and Bangando homes incorporate architectural elements drawn from each other's traditional house styles. The two groups also share cultural traditions with each other. In our brief time in Dioula, we were treated to two celebrations that included singing and dancing from both Baka and Bangando performers—to appreciative gatherings composed of both groups.

Our first lesson from Lobéké draws on this experience of the Bangando and the Baka to teach us about our own lives as members of ethnic communities: it is that, if we resist the temptation to stereotype others even as we also cherish our own particular traditions, we open up the prospect of learning from our differences.

This lesson sounds deceptively simple. It is, however, a tough one to get right. While we are liberated to celebrate our particularity, we do so in a pluralistic setting that calls for respect and even appreciation for the traditions of our neighbors. This respect and appreciation need not be—and, in the context of a university like Columbia, should not be—uncritical. But critical and self-critical though they be, mutual respect and appreciation are crucial if we are to learn from our differences within an intentionally inclusive community.

A second lesson from Lobéké concerns our lives as actors in the world economy. No one can travel from the United States to Cameroon without a vivid sense of the economic contrast between the two countries. Despite Cameroon's substantial natural resources, the vast majority of its people are extremely poor when income and economic wealth are measured by American standards.

The home of the family with whom our daughter lives provides one indicator of the standard of living in the area. Their stick, mud, and thatch house is about twenty years old, and it is showing signs of its age. The family decided to expand its space, this time moving one notch higher on the hierarchy of housing: three rooms of all wood construction, except for the mud floor and the tin roof. Stephanie agreed to share in the cost of the new structure. Covering half of the expense amounted to $200, when the rate for a hotel room at the Hilton in the capital of Yaoundé is $270 a night.

I note the scale and cost of housing, not to suggest that Bangando families are to be pitied, but simply to focus our attention on the dramatic disparity between what we and they take for granted. That difference almost unavoidably introduces an asymmetry into relations between us and them that informs every interaction. Most damagingly, the enormous contrast in available resources may lead to a counterproductive and in the end destructive dependency.

This dependency is evident dozens of times every day. At the geopolitical level, conservation areas are established only if governments from the developed world or international nongovernmental organizations provide financial backing. Similarly, less-than-robust economic activity is attributed to the failure of trading partners to provide adequate subsidies. At the very personal and local level, an injury or infection that traditional healing methods cannot cure may call for intervention that only modern transportation and medicine can provide.

Our second lesson from Lobéké is that the best and maybe the only way to counter what all too quickly becomes a vicious cycle of dependency is to reach a more balanced development and distribution of resources. The challenge all of us together face is, therefore, to design economic development programs that provide assistance without reinforcing dependency. Only such programs can over the long haul lead to a more balanced generation and sharing of resources.

A third lesson from Lobéké is closely related to this need for long-term programs designed to reach a more balanced development and distribution of resources: it is that we exercise more effectively our responsibility for human impacts on the environment.

The activity of extracting wood products from the forest provides an illuminating prism for viewing this environmental responsibility. Logging companies are a very visible presence in Cameroon. Except for a hundred or so kilometers of paved highway from Yaoundé, we traveled—for two twelve-hour days in each direction—only on dirt roads that logging companies maintained just enough to allow their enormous trucks to transport their products: huge loads of mahogany and other hardwood logs and, less often, already milled lumber. In the dry season the roads, and the villages en route, are blanketed with thick clouds of red dust, only to become seas of mud and standing water in the rainy season.

There are long-term plans to designate the entire region of the Lobéké Forest as a conservation area stretching from southeastern Cameroon into both the Republic of the Congo and the Central African Republic. But for now, large tracts of southeastern Cameroon are leased as logging concessions to international timber companies. The infrastructure of roads, the presence of the latest and biggest logging equipment, the development of small-scale local industry in the form of sawmills, and the provision of employment, education, and health care are all quite impressive—as is the large number of gigantic trees being extracted from the forest, most of which have grown there for hundreds of years.

Immersion in the forest is certainly one way of getting a vivid sense of just how massive is its capacity to absorb the impact of human activity. Even with all of our equipment, we humans are still very small in this setting. And yet as massive as is the capacity of nature to absorb the damage we inflict, it is not limitless. The lesson we need to learn is therefore straightforward: our exploitation of natural resources must be restrained to levels that are sustainable over the long haul.

I am acutely aware that each of these three lessons from Lobéké almost unavoidably rings hollow here in the great urban plaza of an international university in a sophisticated and sometimes cynical global city. Of course we must learn from our differences even as we cherish our own particular traditions as members of ethnic communities. Of course we must support economic development programs that provide assistance without reinforcing dependency. Of course we must restrain exploitation of natural resources to levels that the environment can sustain. So what else is new?

But despite my awareness that these three lessons must sound like little more than clichés, I venture to state them because I am convinced that they are crucial for all of us as members of ethnic communities, as actors in the world economy, and as participants in our planetary ecosystem. One of the advantages of viewing the global scene from the perspective of Lobéké is that we can recognize how often we dismiss uncomfortable truths by characterizing them as sentimental truisms. If we are to avoid that trap, we must consider each of these lessons as worthy of our collective attention and action.

Certainly action as well as attention is required. To state each lesson in the abstract is easy enough. But to cultivate informed respect for both one's own and other traditions, to design concrete programs that press toward a more balanced development and distribution of resources, to devise institutional mechanisms and multilateral policies that contribute to achieving environmental sustainability—to move toward all of these goals will require extensive effort over multiple generations. That is why learning these lessons from Lobéké and pursuing the goals they imply are worthy of our collective energy, imagination, and intelligence as you commence from this university.

I hope and expect that what you have learned at Columbia will contribute to your capacity to make a difference in addressing such issues. We who have had the privilege of working with you during your time here look forward to reports of your continuing effectiveness. On behalf of all of us, I wish you all the best—for all of our sake.

# PART 2
*Action for Inclusion*

# 7 Local Conflicts as a Global Challenge

ON NO SET OF ISSUES is the imperative to work toward inclusive communities more pressing than the changing shape and character of conflict in recent decades. This new face of war is indeed a global challenge. Yet this global challenge has its roots in a myriad of local conflicts. To understand and respond to the global challenge, we must recognize how much local conflicts of today no longer fit the pattern of war that for more than three hundred years has dominated at least Western conceptions of human history.

## The New Face of War

Across the globe, the face of war is new in comparison to what we in the West have known for most of the modern era—from roughly the middle of the seventeenth century to the latter part of the twentieth century. The beginning of this period is marked by the Peace of Westphalia, the agreement that ended Europe's Thirty Years' War in 1648. This treaty in effect recognized the demise of the Holy Roman Empire and the advent of historical dominance by nation-states.

Transnational forces, including the religious allegiances that had helped to fuel the thirty years of conflict, were subordinated to the state. In the aftermath of the seemingly endless fighting, there were calls for tolerance and even some allowance for dissent. But, at least initially, the heads of

---

This chapter incorporates materials developed in a number of talks, beginning with a lecture at Dartmouth College in September 2004.

state of Europe were accorded the right to determine the religious allegiance of their subjects. Over time, secular societies like France after the French Revolution and pluralistic countries like the United States rejected the model of a state religion, though even then the authority of the government to set the ground rules for religious expression was taken for granted.

This modern era continued through World War II. Then the emergence of competition between two multinational systems in the Cold War attenuated the supremacy of the nation-state. At the same time, the serial conflicts in Vietnam over a period of almost three decades anticipated some of the features of the emerging new face of war. Finally, the collapse of the Soviet Union and the emergence of a single superpower have led first to an assertion of unilateral force over against established governments and then in turn to a reassertion of the prerogatives of nation-states.

We can debate when this modern era of war ended. Those of us who delight in symmetry might opt for the three decades of conflict in Vietnam to serve as the counterpart of the Thirty Years' War. But whenever precisely we date the end of this modern era, for more than three hundred years the historical dominance of the nation-state resulted in a pattern of conducting war that we still often take for granted. In this pattern, war is fought between two or more nation-states, with only the occasional exception like the American Civil War. Over against such interminable conflicts as the Thirty Years' War, the duration of the fighting is measured in years, not decades. Finally, conventions of war have been elaborated with the intention of focusing the fighting—and therefore the casualties—on combatants. While there were again exceptions, conspicuously toward the end of World War II, these conventions were widely respected, with the result that in the typical war of the modern era on the order of 90 percent of casualties were soldiers and only about 10 percent were civilians.

On each of these counts, many current cases of conflict conform to a quite different pattern. Rather than wars between nation-states, most contemporary conflicts are fought between factions within nominally unified countries. The duration of the fighting is frequently decades long. The ratio between civilian and combatant casualties is very different and in quite a few cases may even be reversed: as many as 90 percent of the deaths in these wars are of those not directly involved in fighting, while soldiers may account for as few as 10 percent of those who die. To see this new face of war, we need look no further than recent conflicts in Afghanistan, the Democratic Republic of Congo, and Sudan.

## Displaced Persons, Uprooted Communities

Among the horrors that are inescapable in this new face of war are the enormous numbers of uprooted individuals, families, and whole communities. Right now there are over fifty million displaced people in the world, about one-third of them officially recognized as refugees because they have crossed an international border and the other two-thirds as so-called "internally displaced persons" (IDPs) because they are still within their own country. To bring that number home, it is roughly equal to the populations of the metropolitan areas of Boston, New York, Chicago, Minneapolis, Seattle, Portland, San Francisco, Los Angeles, Houston, Dallas, Atlanta, Washington, D.C., and Baltimore—all added together.

These millions of displaced people figure in our sense of dislocation worldwide: throngs of people who clutch their belongings as they flee conflict; long lines of supplicants who wait for water, food, shelter, or application papers; circles of family members who rejoice as they are reunited after years of separation.

A challenge to which we in the world community must rise is to address the problems these more than fifty million displaced people are confronting every day and to work with them to achieve durable solutions. The International Rescue Committee is focused on meeting that challenge. I therefore invite you to look with me at this tough set of issues from the perspective of the IRC's activities worldwide.

The International Rescue Committee was founded in 1933 at the suggestion of Albert Einstein. Its first governing board included John Dewey, Reinhold Niebuhr, and other luminaries. It had a straightforward mission: to rescue refugees from Europe and to help them get resettled in the United

States. To that end it had operations in Europe to expedite escape from Germany and countries under Nazi occupation and an office in New York to assist refugees in becoming reestablished in this country.

The IRC continues to assist refugees who are admitted for resettlement in this country. We have twenty-two offices across the United States for this purpose. It is exhilarating work. Because many of our resettlement staff are themselves former refugees, they are very adept at exercising the tough love required to stimulate and support newcomers to restart their lives in a matter of months. We are proud of the fact that in the more than eighty years of our history, the IRC has helped hundreds of thousands of refugees become productive Americans.

After 9/11, the numbers of refugees admitted for resettlement in the United States declined precipitously. In recent years that number has rebounded. But even though the number admitted has again reached the pre-9/11 presidentially mandated ceiling of seventy thousand, fewer than 2 out of every 1,000 displaced individuals have any hope of being resettled in the United States, which in turn requires that the 998 out of every 1,000 must find other ways of coping.

This arithmetic—that 998 out of every 1,000 displaced individuals have no prospect of finding a new home in the United States—is why the IRC not only continues the work of resettling refugees here but also is committed to the equivalent of resettlement in forty countries around the world. Of the refugees who are not admitted to the United States, a small number will be resettled in other countries. Although the IRC has not historically been involved in the process of resettlement in developed countries other than the United States, our London office, which was formed to support our international programs, has also advised the British government as it reexamines its asylum policies. But in any case, for the vast majority of displaced people, certainly well over 99 percent, a durable solution to the problem of displacement takes one of two forms: either integration into the place to which they have fled or voluntary repatriation to the home from which they have been uprooted.

The International Rescue Committee works on all fronts of this battle for durable solutions. To illustrate the range of our efforts, I will refer to refugees from Afghanistan as an example. For over thirty years, we have assisted Afghan refugees who have resettled in the United States. Virtually all of them are great success stories: proud Americans who also remain deeply interested in Afghanistan. For the past thirty-five years, we have also been working with Afghan refugees in Pakistan. We first became engaged when the Soviet invasion in 1979 began to generate large numbers of displaced people. All through the tumult of more than three decades we have worked with Afghan refugees in Pakistan, and for the past twenty-seven years we have also had programs operating inside Afghanistan itself. As a result, we have been well positioned as large numbers of refugees have returned voluntarily to their homeland.

Once again, the numbers are illuminating. Over more than two decades, about twelve thousand Afghan refugees have been resettled in the United States, roughly a quarter of them with the assistance of the IRC. During that period the number of Afghan refugees reached a peak of more than eight million in the early 1990s—about seven hundred times as many as resettled in the United States. The vast majority of those millions of refugees fled to either Iran or Pakistan. Most have now returned to their homeland. But not all of the refugees who do not resettle to a third country will return. Instead of voluntary repatriation, perhaps as many as two million will opt for local integration, especially in the ethnically similar Northwest Frontier Province of Pakistan.

The IRC has been actively engaged with refugee settlements in this region from the beginning of our time in Pakistan. The children who have grown up in these settlements are now adults who have never lived in Afghanistan. Their villages are relatively well integrated into the social and economic patterns of that part of Pakistan. In some respects, notably in education and health care, their situation is more favorable than that of the local Pakistanis. We have, therefore, increasingly opened up access to our programs to the Pakistani population as well, so as to facilitate the full acceptance of Afghan refugees into what has become their new home.

The IRC certainly did not work with all of these Afghan refugees. But over the years we have assisted hundreds of thousands of uprooted people both in Pakistan and in Afghanistan. In every case our governing intention is to develop the capacity of the displaced so that they can restart their lives—the equivalent for them of the situation of resettlement in the United States for a small fraction of the total.

As in most of the countries where we are active, our programs include water and sanitation, housing, health care, and education. The educational programs have been especially important, because they have prepared a generation of leaders, some who have been in Afghanistan for years and others who are now returning from Pakistan. Inside Afghanistan, the IRC also administered a system of small house-based schools that continued operating even during the rule of the Taliban. We educated girls as well as boys, which the Taliban tolerated because parents insisted on it. Interestingly, the former deputy director for IRC programs in Pakistan and Afghanistan, Haneef Atmar, was the minister for rural development in the new government formed just after the Taliban-dominated government was defeated. And Hamid Karzai, the first president of this new government, himself once taught English in our school for Afghan refugees in Peshawar, Pakistan, as he proudly reminded me when we met in Kabul in 2002.

In the early years our programs inside Afghanistan focused intensively on developing the infrastructure that returning refugees require. During my visits I found it enormously gratifying to see the water and sanitation systems that we had cooperated with Afghans to develop and to hear again and again how important the education received in IRC schools has been. It was a special pleasure to have local residents point to apple orchards and to stands of fast-growing poplars used for ceiling beams in the mud-brick houses we helped to build and be told that the IRC provided the seedlings planted fifteen or more years earlier.

One initiative that focuses directly on the need to establish both a viable national government and sustainable local communities is called the National Solidarity Program, funded primarily by the World Bank. The IRC is one of the implementing partners for this program and has two further connections to its development: first, the driving force for the initiative in the Afghan government was our former IRC staff member Haneef Atmar, in his role as minister for rural development; and second, the IRC sent a team from Rwanda to advise on the design of the program based on a similar effort in that country. In any case, the program as it is being implemented in Afghanistan begins with empowering local village councils and then works to provide national and international support for development priorities established through deliberations at that level.

Afghanistan is certainly not safely beyond the turmoil of the past. It is still on a knife edge and could again fall back into chaos. That is why it is crucial that the United States and other developed countries follow through on the assistance we have promised. If we do, and if the Afghans rise to the enormous challenges they still face, we will be able to take some satisfaction on our shared achievement.

As for the IRC, Afghanistan illustrates our strategy for building local capacity. Our staff in Afghanistan is now composed almost exclusively of Afghans—some 650 persons—together with a handful of expatriates, for an IRC-Afghanistan team that is 99 percent Afghan nationals. And this team in turn works with some 1,500 other Afghans employed by local nongovernmental organizations that we have helped create over the years and to which we subcontract many of the water, sanitation, agricultural development, health, and education projects that we undertake. That is a ratio of more than four hundred Afghans per expatriate—an infrastructure of talented workers that will remain when the IRC departs, which we will.

I have focused on the situation of those uprooted in and from Afghanistan to illustrate the multiple ways the International Rescue Committee, as a representative of the international community, addresses the challenges posed when local conflicts produce large numbers of displaced people. I could of course adduce a distressingly large number of further examples. But instead of multiplying case studies, I would rather enlist other relevant examples to help us reflect on lessons I think we can learn from our involvement in the aftermath of such local conflicts.

## 1. Beyond Dependence to New Capacity

The first lesson is one that we who work in humanitarian relief and development organizations must learn. It arises from the fact that our initial involvement in any given situation often results from responding to an emergency or a crisis. The lesson is that we must from the very beginning of our intervention resist the temptation to foster dependence on the part of those victimized by conflict. Put positively, we must focus at the outset on building the capacity of those with whom we work to begin their lives anew.

This lesson is, of course, much easier to state than to exemplify. In the heat of an emergency, the first priority unavoidably is to seek to meet immediate needs. When the death toll from readily preventable diseases rises sharply—for example, from diarrhea or cholera—what is immediately required is potable water and rehydration therapy rather than a long-term plan for rehabilitation. Yet even though the most pressing demands for assistance must be met, the danger that providing short-term help may undermine long-term self-subsistence must be avoided.

In recent years the efforts of the IRC's emergency response teams in Chad and the Darfur region of Sudan illustrate how tough it is to avoid this danger. There were over a million displaced people in Darfur. Another two hundred thousand refugees crossed the border from Darfur into Chad. Forced to flee from their native villages, uprooted people had dispersed over large areas of western Sudan and eastern Chad. They were mostly women and children, because the men were systematically killed by the government-armed militia who covet their land. For security and to be able to provide food, water, and shelter, there seems no viable alternative to gathering the refugees and internally displaced persons into settlements or camps. The IRC worked with the United Nations and other agencies to do just that. We of course knew that we must not allow this short-term expedient to become long-term maintenance in camps, which in effect would aid and abet ethnic cleansing in Darfur. Yet to insist that the uprooted return immediately to their villages would have not only invited further slaughter and rape but also starvation and disease because the planting season had passed and the wells had been deliberately poisoned with human corpses and animal carcasses.

So I do not underestimate the difficulty of following the advice that this first lesson teaches. There are perverse incentives that encourage passive maintenance of refugees in camp settings: free food and shelter for the refugees themselves; a revenue stream for host governments; jobs for the local population, which therefore has an interest in proscribing local employment of camp residents; contracts for international agencies that manage the camps; the release of the home country from responsibility to reintegrate those who have fled. Instead of deploying funds in ways that reinforce these perverse incentives, all of us must work in every way we can to move expeditiously from sustenance that fosters dependence to building the capacity to begin anew. That requires firm advocacy to the United Nations, to countries that host refugees, and to governments that have allowed their residents to be displaced. It also requires programs that afford opportunities for education, training, and employment so that the uprooted are prepared to be productive members of the communities to which they return or into which they are integrated locally.

## 2. Sound Government as Crucial

The second lesson is less directly concerned with humanitarian relief and development organizations. But even if it has wide-ranging ramifications, it comes into sharp focus in the settings in which such groups work. This lesson is that communities at all levels, up to and including governments, are crucial for human flourishing—and at times even for survival.

In executing my responsibilities at the International Rescue Committee, I visited dozens of countries that illustrate the disastrous consequences of the collapse of communities, to a significant degree because of a record of persistently bad government. The Democratic Republic of Congo is a vivid example. I will refer in some detail to this particular case to exemplify a more general pattern, in part because I have access to sobering data that the IRC has painstakingly gathered over more than half a decade.

The disastrous state of what is now the Democratic Republic of Congo (DRC) has a long history that includes voracious colonial exploitation dating back to the last quarter of the nineteenth century under King Leopold II of Belgium and the corrupt postcolonial rule of Mobutu Sese Seko. But its most recent turmoil stems from 1994, when many of the perpetrators of genocide in Rwanda fled into eastern Zaire. By 1996 violence and unrest led Rwanda and Uganda to join with Zairian rebel groups to establish control over eastern Zaire. In a matter of months these invading forces, together with their Zairian allies, overthrew the government and installed a replacement, which renamed Zaire the Democratic Republic of Congo. Rwandan and Ugandan forces then withdrew briefly, only to return in August 1998, invoking the need to control the security on their borders. Over the next six months, other forces became involved, with the result that by early 1999 troops from seven countries in the region, allied with various Congolese factions, were fighting in the five eastern provinces of the DRC.

The fighting was intense and continuous from August 1998 until February 2001, when an accord between Rwanda and the DRC resulted in significantly decreased tensions and the beginning of pulling back troops from the frontlines. This accord in turn prepared the way for peace talks in South Africa. An agreement in principle was signed in Pretoria in July 2002, followed by a framework for power sharing and the withdrawal of Rwandan troops in December 2002.

During precisely this period, the IRC was conducting a series of surveys in the DRC. These surveys recorded a very basic measure of health, namely mortality rates. Because of the parallels in timing, they provide powerful documentation of the disastrous human consequences of such long-term conflicts.

Using standard sampling techniques, an IRC team conducted surveys in 2000 and 2001. Based on the data, the team—led by epidemiologist Les Roberts—estimated that approximately 2.5 million deaths occurred in eastern DRC above the million or so that would have been expected under stable non-conflict circumstances. (The 2.5 million number is an approximation because a sensitivity analysis of plausible assumptions about the baseline mortality rate and the extrapolations inherent in the estimation process in fact yield a range of 2.1 to 3.2 million excess deaths.)

In 2002, the IRC team conducted a third survey. This survey estimated mortality for the first ten months of that year—the period during which a ceasefire was established and both United Nations observers and humanitarian relief agencies were able to gain greater access to populations victimized by the conflict. This third survey also included comparative data from a parallel survey of western DRC.

The third survey for 2002 reported more bad news: the excess mortality rate continued to be awful. For the entire period of the war—from August 1998 to the end of 2002—the IRC estimate of deaths above the expected baseline level is 3.3 million. This death toll exceeded that of the Biafran conflict and is therefore the highest total for any war in Africa. Indeed, it is higher than the total for any war anywhere since World War II. To put the point sharply, this death toll is the equivalent in loss of life of a World Trade Center disaster every day for over three years. For those of us who experienced the impact of 9/11, this comparison cannot but shock us into a sense of the enormity of this tragedy: total deaths that equal the number of lives lost in the Twin Towers—but every day for more than three years running.

Yet as awful as this news is, there was also good news in the 2002 survey. Comparing the figures in the third survey to those in the first two, the mortality rate declined by more than a third. The rate is still extremely high—and still higher than the rate for the western part of the country, which has experienced far less violent conflict. But the peace accord, the introduction of 4,400 United Nations observers, the withdrawal of Rwandan troops, and greater access for humanitarian assistance all contributed to a reduced level of violent conflict. While the eastern DRC does not by international standards have an effectively functioning government, and while the relatively subdued level of conflict could certainly explode again (as it did in the Ituri region in the spring of 2003 and near the Rwandan border in the spring of 2004), even this limited peace is correlated with a significant decrease in mortality rates.

In the intervening years, the DRC has experienced both brief times of further advances in peace and extended periods of terrible resurgent fighting. The challenge is to continue the modestly positive trajectory documented in the IRC surveys. To do so requires the further consolidation of protection and security. It also calls for the positive provision for adjudicating conflicting claims and establishing social order acceptable to opposed parties. In short, it entails the authority that sound governance provides to well-ordered communities—a lesson that can be generalized to dozens of other conflict and post-conflict settings around the world.

This lesson is especially important for us Americans to learn. Criticism of the state has a long and honorable history here. None of us has much patience with the bureaucracy and red tape that frequently characterize government programs. But what at times has been a useful and even necessary stimulus to improvement or efficiency or even elimination of excess has in recent years too often become a denigration of government as such. For any of us who spend time in failed states, this refusal to recognize the crucial role of government in establishing the order that our common life requires is a serious mistake. Put positively, to address the challenges of conflict situations worldwide, we must embrace the positive role of government in building communities that are stable and secure.

## 3. Prevention Rather than Intervention

The third lesson we need to learn is the most basic of the three and follows directly from this acknowledgement of the crucial role of government in establishing ordered communities: it is that catastrophe prevention is vastly preferable to emergency intervention.

Prevention strategies will necessarily proceed on multiple fronts. For example, trade policies must more consistently deliver on promises that poor as well as rich countries benefit from globalization. Here there is much room for improvement. The most recent major international trade agreement, called the Uruguay Round, was concluded in 1994. (I am not counting the relatively minor achievements of the multiple Doha Round meetings, including the most recent December 2013 session in Bali, Indonesia.) The Uruguay Round set out a straightforward bargain: developed countries would reduce their agricultural subsidies and developing countries would in return lower their tariffs on imports. Developing countries have taken significant steps to meet their side of the bargain by halving their average tariffs. In contrast, developed countries have reneged on their pledges: subsidies in recent years have constituted almost 40 percent of the value of Western farm output—about the same as when the Uruguay Round was launched.

I concede that these gross metrics oversimplify the situation. There are products that developing countries import that do not compete with local production, and that therefore benefit their consumers and perhaps even foster economic growth. But there are also commodities that are significantly subsidized and that in effect thereby compete unfairly with what developing countries themselves produce and could export to generate revenue. Cotton is the best example. The export potential of African cotton growers is systematically undermined even though the cost of producing superb cotton there is lower. The result is the undermining of the local production capacity crucial for development.

The cost to developing countries of this failure to abide by global trade agreements is substantial. For agriculture alone, Western export subsidies and trade barriers amount to more than five times the total of Western foreign aid. Manufactured goods from the developing world also face tariff barriers that are on average four times as high as those levied on products from the industrialized world. To put it gently, this state of affairs is hard to defend, especially if we are serious in seeking to anticipate and prevent conflict through orderly development.

Another arena, and one in which the global community (including associations of developing countries like the African Union) has contributed effectively to conflict prevention, is in providing peacekeeping forces. Here the United Nations has often been the lead, but other coalitions of nations (NATO and the African Union, for example) also contribute. The result is that conflict is very significantly less likely to reignite in situations in which peacekeepers are on the ground—a very basic illustration of preventive action rather than emergency response.

Along with at least leveling the playing field in trade and serious investment in peacekeeping forces, the developed world must also increase foreign assistance for investment in basic health care and education. At the

World Food Summit in 1996, advanced industrialized countries agreed on setting the goal that each would contribute 0.7 percent of its gross national income for international assistance—a target that had first been set in the 1960s. By the early years of the twenty-first century, five countries had reached or surpassed this goal: Denmark, Norway, Sweden, the Netherlands, and Luxembourg, though the average for the twenty-two developed countries as a group was far short of the mark. At that point, the country that ranked dead last on this measure—twenty-second out of twenty-two—was the United States. There is no magic in this figure. Indeed, as some economists have argued, it is based on data that are outdated. Yet it remains a powerful focal point for concentrating attention on the inadequacies of the support provided for international relief and development.

In March 2002 more than fifty heads of state and other leaders met in Monterrey, Mexico, to address the imperative of increasing development assistance. Just before those meetings, President George W. Bush announced that the United States would increase foreign economic assistance by 50 percent over three years. After a decade of stagnant development budgets, that would have been a most welcome step in the right direction—if the funds had in fact been appropriated, which turned out to be only very partially the case. In subsequent years, despite positive rhetoric, the United States is still near the bottom of developed countries in terms of this measure of commitment to assistance for international relief and development.

What is striking in this situation is not only the fact that the United States ranks near the bottom but also the extent of national self-deception on the issue. Polls consistently show that most of us think we as a nation are more generous than other countries in providing economic aid to developing countries. I think that there are two considerations that help to explain this discrepancy between the actual facts and our sense of ourselves. The first is that Americans give generously through private or nongovernmental agencies, a resource not included in international comparisons of official development assistance. And second, as I noted in my pointed remarks to

Rice University students in chapter 6, our own past performance was in fact far more generous than the more recent pattern.

To note again figures that I cited in chapter 6, in the late 1940s, at the height of the Marshall Plan, the fraction of the U.S. federal budget committed to foreign assistance was over 18 percent, an astonishingly large proportion. As a percentage of gross national income, it was 2.6 percent. By the early 1960s, this percentage had dropped by a factor of seven to 0.6 percent. And today the figure is a little over 0.2 percent, one-third of the level in the early 1960s and one-twelfth of the level in 1948.

However we explain the discrepancy between our sense of our own generosity as a nation and the actual facts, we need to focus our energy and attention on rectifying the situation so that the United States does closer to its fair share of the investment in basic health care and education that are crucial for sustainable development worldwide. I am acutely aware that statistical measures like percentages of gross national income or fractions of the federal budget can be off-putting. To bring such dry statistics to life, I reiterate the invitation I extended in chapter 6 to think in terms of a ten-dollar bill as the total gross national income of a country: of that ten dollars, the most generous nation, Norway, gives about a dime for development assistance, while the United States gives only two cents—two cents out of ten dollars! Even if we add in private donations, that would be only another few pennies, for a total of less than a nickel out of ten dollars. That is how feeble our current effort is.

We can and should do more. In this respect our closest ally, the United Kingdom, is setting an example that we need to emulate. Even though the United Kingdom has not been among the leading countries in the relative scale of its development aid, it has been significantly more generous than the United States—about two and a half times as generous, again measured as a percentage of gross national income. Under the leadership of Prime Minister Tony Blair, the United Kingdom committed itself to almost tripling its 2002 level of assistance. Successive governments have maintained this commitment. Even when facing the austerities following the economic crisis after the collapse of financial markets at the end of the first decade of the twenty-first century, the British government insisted that it would not reduce development assistance.

The United States must do likewise. If we rise to the challenge of approximating the level of commitment of Norway, Denmark, Sweden, the Netherlands, Luxembourg, and (prospectively) the United Kingdom, we could potentially have a tremendously positive impact on the forward movement of the developing world. If this increased investment is carefully targeted in basic health care and education, if it includes incentives for governments in developing countries to shoulder their responsibilities more effectively, and if it is combined with fair global trade agreements, the result could be a major transformation in the developing world—in particular in sub-Saharan Africa—over the next generation.

This challenge is the great opportunity we have before us. Organizations like the International Rescue Committee will continue to intervene in emergency situations that conflicts generate and to work from the beginning of their interventions for durable solutions to the problems they encounters. They will also press for local and national governments to assume their responsibilities for the security that communities require to flourish. Finally, they are and will continue to be staunch advocates for more adequate levels of investment in the foreign assistance that can help to prevent conflict before it demands outside interventions. All of these efforts require more resources and deserve more support because they are crucial to achieving a world that recognizes the imperative for inclusive communities as the only viable alternative to endless conflict.

# 8  People on the Move

PERHAPS THE MOST POSITIVE way to think about the displaced persons and uprooted communities that result from current conflicts is to see these victims of war as people on the move toward what might become new prospects for living fulfilled lives. These uprooted people often have very few resources: they flee with only what they can carry and all too frequently have little education or transferable work experience. Yet they are among the vast array of migrants searching for new opportunities. People on the move yearn for a new place that can be home, even if "home" in the end is the area from which they have fled once it is safe to return. In this sense, internally displaced persons and refugees quite literally embody the quest for inclusive communities.

## The Context of Globalization

I noted in the introduction and again in chapter 2 that both of my parents were immigrants to the United States. Their closest friends were also immigrants. I grew up taking for granted that my parents and their friends—as

---

This chapter draws on material from my speech "People on the Move: Refugees in the Context of Globalization," delivered as the Emma Lazarus Lecture on International Flows of Humanity at Columbia University in March 2006; from a lecture at the Yale Divinity School entitled "The Challenge of Immigration: Framing a New American Conversation," delivered in May 2008 and published in revised form as "Sending, Receiving, Embracing: The Pulse of Global Immigration," *Reflections* 93, no. 2 (Fall 2008), 23–29; and "People on the Move," a talk given at a joint program of the Houston Forum and the Asia Society-Texas in April 2003.

well as my schoolmates, many of whose parents were also immigrants from a great variety of places—were full members of our society. On occasion I was reminded of differences within this membership. For example, when I was about eight, a friend asked how come my father spoke so funny. For as long as I can remember, perhaps beginning with that question, I have had a fascination with accents. But I was, on that occasion, taken aback at the suggestion that my father, who had a strong South German accent all of his life, spoke any differently from any other American.

By the time I was born, my parents had moved across the Hudson River from New York to New Jersey. Virtually all of their friends had also moved in every direction out from New York City. As a result, the only practical place to meet (at least for larger gatherings) was back in the city. In my early years I therefore had many occasions to travel across the Pulaski Skyway and through the Holland Tunnel to the McBurney YMCA on Twenty-third Street, where my parents and their friends and families met and celebrated festive occasions.

I mention this obscure fact only because it allows me to underscore how pleased and honored I was to be appointed the Emma Lazarus Lecturer on International Flows of Humanity. As those who on occasion venture across the Hudson River know, the route I described approaches Manhattan very near the Statue of Liberty. So I feel a sense of physical as well as family connection to the eloquent words from "The New Colossus," the poem written by Emma Lazarus carved into the base of the Statue of Liberty: "Give me your tired, your poor, your huddled masses yearning to breathe free."

The almost unavoidable context for any contemporary examination of the issues of migration is the press of globalization. I use "globalization" to refer in summary form to the complex social processes that put us more frequently, more speedily, and more intensively in contact with others all over the world. Increasingly we take those processes for granted. After all, rapid transportation over great distances and virtually instantaneous, relatively inexpensive telecommunications have been with us for a couple of generations now. But the frequency, the pace, and the intensity have accelerated in recent years, as we have absorbed the cumulative impact of more extensive international radio and television news coverage, cheaper transportation and telecommunications, and the explosion of e-mail and Internet usage.

Globalization entails increasingly efficient transfers of money, goods and services, and ideas across social and cultural borders. We take international financial transactions more or less for granted even though the magnitude of capital flows is staggering in comparison with even the recent past. Similarly, while international trade is scarcely a new development, the scale of the global movement of goods and services is unprecedented. Likewise in the case of ideas, the global impact of communications, media, and even cultural expression and intellectual property of all kinds has reached new heights.

Yet the movement of money, goods and services, and ideas is relatively straightforward compared to the movement of people. Here too our situation is certainly not altogether novel, most notably in the United States and especially in places like New York City, with its proud tradition of welcoming newcomers. But the world as a whole is confronting the realities of more people on the move, from more different directions and with more diverse motivations than ever before in human history.

Our American experience as a nation of immigrants serves us well as we rise to meet this new set of challenges. In fact, it gives us a significant advantage in comparison to countries with more homogeneous populations. This comparative advantage has allowed the United States to develop a relatively open labor market that can attract needed workers from outside the country and, over time, integrate them into our society.

The immigration of workers who seek new opportunities is the motivation of the movement of people that is the easiest to accommodate. It is therefore all the more regrettable that the United States has become significantly less welcoming in recent years, especially in contrast to the other developed economies that have increasingly recognized the need for open borders. Yet even in this case, many developed countries have not been as successful as the United States. Think of the persistent failure of Germany to accept Turkish and Greek guest workers as full citizens or even in many cases their children who are born and live their entire lives in Germany, though this pattern seems finally to be changing. Or consider the marginalized status of generations of Koreans in Japan.

Especially in the context of the excesses of recent political rhetoric, I do not need to emphasize the stresses that may accompany the presence of diverse cultural traditions. But nostalgia for some mythic monocultural past is a loss—for the United States and increasingly for the rest of the world. On this set of issues, the United States, the United Kingdom, Canada, and Australia show more promise than France or Germany. Similarly, an India that incorporates its large Muslim minority is a better bet for long-term success than a Pakistan that defines itself as exclusively Muslim. When people are on the move worldwide, to accept—if not embrace—the challenges of ethnic, religious, and cultural diversity is a more promising prescription for vitality than to define a nation monoculturally.

While our experience as a nation of immigrants serves us well in incorporating individuals and families who come to the United States for economic opportunity, it is not an adequate guide for the new global situation we face. Even in the case of economic immigrants, the United States has certainly not offered an open door or a welcoming hand. One result is a large influx of illegal immigrants. This influx of immigrants—in particular, of illegal immigrants—constitutes a major policy conundrum for this country. It will therefore rightly figure prominently in our national debates in the years—and decades—ahead. But placing the issue of illegal entry into the United States in the context of global migration calls attention to the extent to which we cannot adequately address the challenge of immigration that faces receiving countries unless we also attend to the underlying dynamics in sending countries. This interplay between sending and receiving countries is crucial for voluntary economic immigrants, whether legal or illegal, as well as for forced migrants, asylum seekers, and refugees.

## The Challenges of Addressing the Needs of Both Sending and Receiving Countries

Because most migrants will not resettle in the United States or other developed countries, it is imperative that we address the needs of the places that generate displaced populations—the sending countries. Only if those needs are addressed do we have any chance of grappling with the challenge of immigration to the United States and other receiving countries. In the preceding chapter, I outlined three lessons from the situations of countries in conflict that generate large numbers of refugees. I will therefore refer to those lessons only briefly before proceeding to the lessons for receiving countries.

One of these lessons is directed towards organizations like the International Rescue Committee. It arises from the fact that their initial involvement in any given situation often results from responding to an emergency or a crisis. The resulting lesson is that every intervention must from the outset take steps to counter the danger of increased dependence on the part of the victims of the conflict. Put positively, we must focus at the start on building the capacity of those with whom we work to rebuild their communities. The aim from the beginning should be to begin lives anew at home rather than to take flight in the face of completely uncertain prospects.

The second lesson for sending countries is that sound governance—from local communities up to and including national governments—is crucial if forced migration is to be avoided. Migration is at least potentially a positive development for the global community. But the template of voluntary emigration and successful immigration is more likely to be realized if and when not only the receiving country but also the sending country has a decent government—a government that has the ability to work with other parties to attract emigrants with badly needed talent to come back home so as to avoid a perverse brain drain.

A third lesson follows directly from the recognition of the crucial role of government in establishing ordered communities: it is that long-term and carefully planned assistance is far more efficient than massive short-term aid in response to an emergency.

These three lessons that are crucial to keep in mind if we, as members of the international community, are going to engage the global issue of migration in ways that address the needs of the sending countries and thereby counter the push factor that drives people from the developing world to the developed world: first, build capacity in countries caught up in conflict; second, focus on encouraging sound government; third, invest in basic healthcare and education and livelihoods.

That brings us to the second set of lessons, those that more directly affect receiving countries. I will again note three examples. The first lesson concerns the imperative that we get our immigration vetting and approvals into some semblance of efficient order instead of allowing fears of world-wide terrorism to paralyze the process or, even worse, letting political calculations lead to deportation procedures that break up families or send immigrants to countries where they have no relationships or connections. The second focuses on the prospect of welcoming connections between immigrants and the places from which they have come. And the third addresses the need for developing a culture of inclusion adequate to the current era of global migration.

## Expedite Immigration and Facilitate Connections to Countries of Origin

We in the United States certainly need to increase the numbers admitted of legal immigrants in general and refugees in particular. But the United States must also streamline its immigration procedures and organize the respective responsibilities of the State Department and the Department of Homeland Security so that the vetting and approval process is less convoluted and protracted. I offer two examples.

Anti-terrorism legislation and regulations enacted by the Treasury Department and the Department of Homeland Security have established that the past provision of "material support" to any armed groups is a disqualification for admission to the United States. "Material support" is defined broadly, with the result that otherwise clearly admissible candidates have been barred. Here are three such instances: a Liberian woman who was beaten and gang-raped by rebels after they killed her father and then was held hostage and forced to wash her captors' clothes; a Karen refugee in Thailand because he had supported resistance to the Myanmar government, which the United States was at the time opposing with sanctions; and a Colombian who paid a "war tax" as a ransom to gain back family members kidnapped by guerilla bands and narcotics traffickers. There is relevant legislation that allows for waivers from the onerous provisions in regard to material support—waivers that have been granted to only a few specific groups. But a more general legislative fix is clearly required.

Another example involves the situation of refugees from Iraq and Syria. This example is a complicated two-step process, in that Syria was a generous host to Iraqi refugees before it began to generate its own enormous numbers of refugees. I have had the opportunity for multiple visits to Iraq, Syria, Jordan, and Turkey in recent years and can report that this complex instance of forced migration is indeed daunting.

To begin with, the situation of Iraqi refugees in Syria and Jordan has too often been quite deplorable. Too many of these refugees from persecution in Iraq have been living in squalid conditions in the poorest parts of Amman and Damascus, not in separate settlements but in and among Jordanians and Syrians. They are not allowed to work legally, in many cases have exhausted their savings, and have limited access to health care and education. The neighboring host countries have borne the brunt of the impact: 500,000 Iraqis in Jordan, which has a total population of about seven million, and 1.5 million in Syria, which has a total population of about twenty-two million.

The challenge has become almost unimaginably harder with the second phase of the tragedy: the civil war raging in Syria. Inside Syria there are now over seven million displaced persons (out of a population of twenty-two million), as well as more than three million refugees in Jordan, Iraq, Lebanon, and Turkey. International aid has been woefully inadequate in assisting the desperate communities inside Syria and also within neighboring countries in coping with this enormous burden of uprooted people.

In response to the first wave of refugees, the United States pledged to admit an increased quota of Iraqis. It even passed legislation to admit Iraqi nationals who worked directly with the U.S. government or American contractors on "special immigrant visas." But these pledges were mired in endless bureaucratic impediments even before the huge expansion of the scope of the problem with the addition of three million refugees from Syria.

The special challenges of anti-terrorism legislation and of refugees from Iraq and Syria highlight the need for the United States to focus on the inadequacies of its own immigration procedures. We need to increase the number of immigrants admitted and expedite the processing of cases. We also must provide more adequate assistance to the host countries of the far larger number of refugees who will not be admitted for resettlement in the United States.

If we view immigration in the context of globalization, not only should we increase the number of immigrants and expedite the process of admission but we should also value the connections between newcomers to America and the places they have left. We all need to be more aware and more vocal about the enormous positive contributions that immigrants have made and continue to make to this country. In particular, we should acknowledge the ways that bilingual and bicultural Americans provide an extremely valuable resource for an all-too provincial country that is struggling to communicate across the globe.

In that spirit, we can and should also recognize and affirm the connections of new Americans to their countries of origin. One indication of those connections is the enormous sum of remittances that migrants around the world send back home. The best estimate of the amount is $300 billion a year. That is triple the total of foreign assistance from all sources worldwide. In addition to the contributions that immigrants are making to their new countries through their labor and their responsible participation in civic life, they are also agents of significant development in their countries of origin. To encourage this process of mutual support is more a privilege than an obligation.

Recognizing and affirming this connection to countries of origin can and should extend even to the immigrants who elicit the most antagonism—namely, those who are in the United States illegally. In the near future, we will need to develop a path to citizenship for such immigrants as well. Before, during, and after that process, solid relationships across the borders of the United States with sending countries should remain a priority.

## Toward a Culture of Inclusion

A final lesson we need to learn concerns how we develop a culture of inclusion that is adequate to this time of massive global migration.

We all know the dominant American narrative. Its motto is *e pluribus unum*. Its metaphor is the melting pot. It is an attractive, compelling story. I personally identify with it to a considerable degree. Indeed, the story of my family illustrates that this account is not just a fondly-told fairy tale.

As I have previously noted, my parents were both immigrants. I spoke German before I learned English, and many close family friends were also immigrants from Germany. In addition, I lived in Germany first as a student and then also as a faculty member during a sabbatical.

But my wife Nancy has long and deep American roots. Nancy traces her family on both sides back to the *Mayflower*. The two families had lived in New England for several centuries until Nancy's father accepted a position in Pennsylvania in 1952. Then in 1956 the family moved to New Jersey, where she and I met in high school.

From Nancy's undiluted, *Mayflower*-originated New England family, the next generation went far afield: Nancy married me, a son of German immigrants; her brother married the daughter of Irish Catholics, a significant departure for the Congregationalist family. Even more remarkable is the story of the generation after, a total of four children including our two daughters: one married the son of Italian Catholic immigrants; the second married a Catholic Singaporean of Chinese and Malay ancestry; the third married a Catholic Puerto Rican; and the fourth married an Indian Sikh.

Every member of this remarkably diverse brood speaks English, in several cases with distinct accents. And every member is fully capable of flourishing in the United States. In this sense they embody the metaphor of the melting pot.

And yet they also express what is new about our situation. The Singaporean has strong ties to his homeland. His family is there. He owns property there. He is fending off job offers to return. The family of the Puerto Rican is bi-located, with homes and business interests in both Florida and Puerto Rico. The parents of the Indian have moved back to India to live there in their retirement. There are thus ongoing connections between the United States and other lands that are completely consistent with our globalized world but different from the pattern of the past.

We have all heard other metaphorical ways of characterizing this new situation. "Salad bowl" and "mosaic" are two. However we describe it, we should make the most of the opportunity that it provides.

If we nurture the connections across countries and cultures, we can all benefit. To refer again to our own family, the next generation—that is, Nancy's and my grandchildren and our grandnephews and grandnieces all speak English as their first language. But this third generation also includes two who speak some and one who speaks a lot of German (our older daughter learned German fluently when our family lived there, and she in turn arranged for her three children to spend a year in German schools during her and her husband's sabbatical in Heidelberg); three who are learning Chinese; three who are growing up speaking Spanish; one who has studied a bit of Japanese (because his mother learned it in school and through living in Japan); and two who are picking up at least a little Hindi.

In addition to encouraging personal connections between U.S. residents and the countries from which their families emigrated, we should also seize the opportunity to regain the high ground on the relations among diverse ethnicities and cultural traditions. We may never again so easily talk about America as the "city on a hill" and as an example for all nations. But we in fact do have a case to make for the resilience and absorptive capacity of the United States, if only we do not press prematurely for the melting pot as the only ideal we cherish.

Consider a couple of examples. At Columbia University, the South Asian Institute brings together students and faculty with personal backgrounds, academic interests, and scholarly competence across an enormous range of study and cultural activity that features India, Pakistan, Bangladesh, Sri Lanka, Nepal, Bhutan, and the Maldives. While the institute focuses on particular traditions, it also allows commonalities across communities to come into view.

Or consider a less academic instance. The Detroit metropolitan area and Dearborn in particular are well known as centers for the settlement of Iraqi immigrants. There are large enough numbers that subsets of Iraqis can practice the religious observances of their communities and cultivate the particular traditions of a variety of ethnic subgroups. Yet, at the same time, there is the prospect of common concerns across what in Iraq can become disabling disagreements. In Dearborn, rather than focusing mainly on differences, Kurds and Arabs, Sunni and Shiite Muslims, even Chaldean Christians and Jews find what they have in common as Iraqis even as they become Iraqi Americans.

As all of us seek to address the challenges of immigration, we should focus again on the impressive resources we have. As I observed at the outset, our experience as a nation of immigrants does serve us well. But even if in the very long run we will be a melting pot, in the shorter term we need to affirm the pluralism of our salad bowl or our mosaic.

I do not believe that there are unmeltable ethnics. But I am convinced that we impoverish ourselves if we move too quickly to insist on a least common denominator. Immigrants who remain loyal to the traditions of their country of origin can still become fully American. The challenge for us is to recognize them and value the way they are our fellow citizens even if their way is not identical to ours. Only this acknowledgement of difference along with an affirmation of what is valuable in the various traditions can move us toward truly inclusive communities.

# 9    Enhancing Local Capacity Globally

A RECURRENT THEME in the previous chapters has been the desirability of building local capacity. In the case of migration, developing opportunities at home will reduce the necessity and even the attraction of seeking opportunity abroad. In the case of international intervention in crises, recruiting and training staff from the affected communities will not only facilitate the delivery of services but also assure that substantial human capital remains in the area after the outside interveners depart—in effect reinforcing the impact of education and employment programs.

To build local capacity on a global scale is an enormous challenge that must be engaged if communities are to be inclusive in the sense of not simply excluding the poor and the marginalized. This challenge certainly confronts developed countries as well as developing countries, especially in those like the United States in which the gap between the top and the bottom of the distribution of income and wealth is growing markedly and is accentuated all the more because of huge differentials in the availability of such crucial resources as education and health care. But because the aim of increasing local capacity has received extensive attention in the international relief and development community, it may be helpful to start there rather than with the need for reform of education, health care, and the tax code of the United States!

## The Efforts of the International Rescue Committee

As I noted in chapter 7, while the International Rescue Committee was originally founded to rescue refugees from the Nazis and help them reestablish their lives and livelihoods in the United States, it now also has operations around the world. While we continue to resettle refugees admitted to the United States, we also work where the vast majority—to repeat, the 998 out of every 1,000 individuals—of displaced people will have to reestablish themselves. That is why building local capacity is such a high priority.

In chapter 7, I noted the National Solidarity Program as an example of our commitment to empowerment at the community or village level. Through this program the IRC has worked in more than 3,600 villages across Afghanistan. We have launched similar programs in other countries—for example, in Rwanda, which served as the template for what we later developed in Afghanistan, and in the Democratic Republic of the Congo, which now has projects in over two thousand villages in South Kivu and Katanga provinces.

Each of these community development programs builds local capacity in multiple ways. It begins with the establishment of a council in each village in which it is active. The council is usually elected, though it can also be constituted through other established consultation processes. It is intended to have a representation across age groups and include women as well as men. This village-based development council identifies its highest priority project and then takes responsibility for overseeing its design and implementation. Along with overall responsibility, the council accepts the assignment of fiscal accountability for the execution of the project.

Here is an anecdote that captures the impact of this local management in Afghanistan. One of the leading figures in the area, who regularly received remuneration for lending his support to private initiatives, informed the chair of the village development council that he would expect his usual payment. The response was that this payment was feasible but that, like all other disbursements, it would have to be recorded and reported in the accounting for all funds received and expended. On reflection, the expediter decided he would not have to be paid after all.

I cannot resist one more anecdote. In the Democratic Republic of Congo, I had the privilege—and, as it turned out, the pleasure—of visiting villages where the IRC was active through its Community-Driven Reconstruction Program with the governor of Katanga Province, Moïse

Katumbi Chapwe. We traveled in his power boat along the Luapula River and were greeted with great enthusiasm and IRC banners at each village, including on the river banks by some where we were not able to stop. One project we visited was an IRC-supervised health center, which the governor found very impressive. I should note that Governor Katumbi is the son of a royal Congolese mother and an Italian Jewish father who was a prominent facilitator of trade between the Congo and Europe. As a result, the governor himself is quite wealthy. His family had donated funds for the building of a health center in a village nearby, and he asked me what the cost had been for the construction of our facility. When I told him, he noted the figure and observed with a smile that in the future he would channel his donations through the IRC!

Along with responsibility for selecting and overseeing the financing of projects, village development councils also orchestrate the contributed labor. The projects selected are almost always a water system, a school, or a health clinic. But sometimes the choice is a larger construction project.

I have an especially vivid recollection of one remarkable instance: a bridge to connect two rural Afghan villages during the rainy season. The overpass was seventy-five yards long and over twenty feet high at the midpoint, with huge arches to allow the water to pass underneath. It was, of course, constructed in the dry season, which is when I visited. Eight years later I can still recall, as if it were yesterday, how proud the village masons were of the majestic stonework in this impressive and beautiful architectural achievement.

The local capacity that those stonemasons embody is already there and is not developed by international aid institutions. Yet enlisting such talent is still a crucial element in enhancing local capacity. For projects in the National Solidarity Program in Afghanistan and analogous programs elsewhere, including the IRC's large Community-Driven Reconstruction Program in the Congo, the usual limit for a contribution from international aid fund is about $60,000. (Occasionally, as in the case of the elevated bridge connection between villages in Afghanistan, we augment that maximum slightly with private funding.) But those public funds from the World

Bank and other international sources in turn leverage local contributions of both labor and materials. The result is an enormous pride in what the villagers together have accomplished.

This overview of our commitment to enhancing local capacity would be incomplete without a consideration of the security of our staff. In extremely tense areas afflicted with ongoing fighting, we do not assign or accept armed security guards for our programs. In the case of Afghanistan, international assistance has typically been extended through provincial reconstruction teams (usually simply referred to as "PRTs"), which are so-called "all of government" entities but are in fact led by military officials. The IRC has consistently declined to accept any aid through that delivery mechanism. At the same time, we have often worked in areas deemed to be insecure. In all of the villages in which we are active, the security of our staff depends on the support of the local communities that participate in and benefit from our joint efforts.

It would be wonderful to be able to claim that we have never had security issues, but it sadly would not be true. We had a horrific incident in which four expatriate staff in an education program were shot and killed in August 2008. There were protests in the local Afghan press that good people should not be targeted. There was also never any acceptance of responsibility for the deed or. even a suggestion that the killing resulted from mistaking our staff for an election monitoring team. But all such explanations are very cold comfort to the families and colleagues of the victims, as I know first-hand from my efforts to express sympathy in person in both Kabul and New York.

In the case of the National Solidarity Program, we have on occasion had staff taken captive. In every case except one, we have been able to enlist the assistance of village elders to secure their release. In one case it was a multi-week process that included travel by the elders across the border into Pakistan to meet with senior Taliban authorities, but it, like other such incidents, ended with the release of our staff without any payment of ransom.

The exception occurred in August 2013 when four members of our young National Solidarity Program engineering staff were taken captive as they were on their way back to the village where they worked after celebrating the holiday of Eid Al-Fitr (to end Ramadan) with their families. We immediately enlisted local village elders to mediate their release, and the process seemed to be proceeding as in the past. But then the four bodies were delivered to the local hospital, all dead from gunshot wounds. We are told that an Afghan army helicopter hovered briefly in the area in which our colleagues were being held captive. Though the helicopter's flight had no connection to our staff, the shooting might have occurred at that time either out of panic or in protest. Any such explanation is again, however, of no comfort to the families of the four young men in their twenties who were contributing to the building of their country. In this case, the Taliban leadership explicitly and publicly dissociated itself from the murders and even personally transmitted messages of sympathy and respect at the victims' funeral ceremonies.

While the IRC was instrumental in the design of the National Solidarity Program, it is certainly not the only implementing partner. Indeed, while the IRC has a presence in more than 3,600 villages, the NSP as a whole has had projects in over thirty thousand villages during the past decade. As a sign for the future, it is therefore deeply troubling that, in contrast to the pattern of the past in which the many thousands of NSP staffers across the country were not targeted, November 2013 saw two further attacks, in these cases on staff of other organizations and not the IRC: one an ambush in which six Afghan staff were killed, and another a remote-controlled bomb that seems to have targeted and in any case killed three further staff members.

The National Solidarity Program and its analogues in other countries illustrate impressively innovative and enormously effective initiatives that focus on enhancing local capacity. While every death is tragic, the number of incidents is a very small fraction of the many thousands of staff members involved. It is of course crucial that villages be ever more vigorous in demonstrating the security that their acceptance provides, and it is also crucial that the World Bank and other donors continue to fund the projects. To close a successful and cost-effective program should not be a serious option.

Enhancing local capacity is a priority across the IRC's programs. Of the more than twelve thousand staff members worldwide, 98 percent of those outside the United States are nationals of the countries where we are operating. The agency-wide intention is to build the capacity of local employees and partners so that their talents and abilities and accomplishments will remain after the IRC leaves—which we will do, even if only after three or more decades. In addition, we are increasingly looking for ways to offer national staff opportunities for education and training so that they can continue to take on the most senior responsibilities in their own countries and also at times join the IRC cadre of expatriate staff in other countries.

My most vivid image for this long-term investment in human capital that is both local and global is from my arrival in Aceh, Indonesia, within weeks of the crisis caused by the tsunami that struck in December 2004. As is the habit of the IRC, we had focused our emergency programs in the remote areas that other agencies determined were unreachable. Because all roads connecting to this region were destroyed, we leased a helicopter to bring in supplies and people—in this instance, including me. As our helicopter landed in Chalang, a remote fishing village otherwise accessible only by a very long sea route, I saw a man in flowing white robes running toward the landing pad. As I emerged from the helicopter, I recognized a colleague from Afghanistan. He greeted me warmly and said, "Mister George, Mister George, I am sure you never thought you would see me here!" He was Akbar Jahn, a water engineer with the IRC in Afghanistan for more than twenty years whom I had met several times in his own country. He had never before been outside of Afghanistan and had now been deployed as a member of our global emergency response team. After quick greetings and pleasantries to out hosts, I went off with Akbar Jahn and other team members to view the gravity-fed water system he had designed, from the collection points at springs on nearby hills to the tap-stand where villagers were filling their buckets with potable water.

Akbar Jahn is back in Afghanistan where he continues to oversee the design and implementation of water systems. He is a talented and dedicated professional. He also is a wonderful representative of the enhanced local capacity that must be developed on a global scale. It is not an easy assignment. But building this network of engaged collaborators is a wonderful instance of developing inclusive communities with common commitments to shared tasks.

## The Federated Model as It Continues to Evolve

While the IRC has devoted substantial attention to the challenge of enhancing global capacity, including at senior levels, we have remained an integrated agency with headquarters in New York City. As I have noted, there are also refugee resettlement offices in twenty-two U.S. cities. In addition, we have regional offices in Nairobi and Bangkok, as well as advocacy, funding, and program support operations in Washington, D.C., Brussels, Geneva, and London. The London office is especially crucial because of its lead role in generating funds from European donors. Yet, though the London office has its own advisory board, there is a single overall governance structure with all fiduciary responsibilities lodged in the headquarters board in New York.

A number of leading international relief and development organizations have evolved a different model, forming a federation of more or less independent chapters rather than a single, integrated institution. Several religious development organizations illustrate this pattern, in particular and on a massive scale, World Vision International. Two other sister agencies that have a lot in common with the IRC and are frequent partners also illustrate the federated model: CARE and Save the Children. The organizational evolution of all three illustrates a concern to move from a more or less monocultural institution to a more pluralistic ethos that includes a significant measure of decentralization in part in order to allow building local capacity.

While World Vision at its start in 1950 was entirely based in the United States, even in its early years it expanded its operations to other countries; it officially became World Vision International in 1977. World Vision International defines itself as a partnership that operates as a federation of independent national offices with three levels of central control: national offices that are registered in their host country as a branch of World Vision International; intermediate-stage national offices that have their own board but must seek approval from World Vision International for major decisions; and national offices that are registered separately in their own countries and have autonomy for internal decisions but must coordinate with World Vision International in keeping with a signed Covenant of Partnership.

Its current complex set of requirements, especially at what it terms the "third level," allows for quite independent national offices, thereby testifying to its efforts to build local capacity even when the result is a considerable loss of control. Recent examples of claims that national offices have departed from international policies that need to be investigated and rectified range from charges of corruption to allegations of evangelization, activities contrary to the clear World Vision International rule against using humanitarian and development aid as a base for proselytization. Despite such occasional conflicts within the larger partnership, World Vision International has continued its efforts at decentralization and empowerment of national agencies.

CARE's development has been less complex, and its regulations at least to this point are less detailed. It has evolved from an American nongovernmental organization providing food aid abroad to a global relief and development network: CARE International, with thirteen members (eight European nations, the United States, Canada, Australia, India, and Thailand) and two affiliate members (Brazil and Peru). Offices within a country are managed by three "lead members"—CARE USA, CARE Canada, and CARE Australia—but there is only a single CARE presence in any country. In keeping with this evolution, CARE, while retaining its wonderful acronym, changed what the letters stand for from "Cooperation for American Remittances in Europe" (a sound description of its activities at the time of its founding in 1945) to "Cooperative for Assistance and Relief Everywhere" (a fair characterization of its activities in the more than eighty countries where it works today). The central secretariat that serves all members is based in Geneva, with branch offices in Brussels and New York. But its members have considerable autonomy, and each is governed by an independent national board. One indication of relative independence is that CARE USA has its headquarters in Atlanta, even though there is a secretariat office in New York. At the same time, CARE International continues to press for greater cohesion among members and a unified management structure for country offices.

On the challenge of building local capacity, Save the Children offers an arresting story. Founded in 1919 in Britain to feed children facing starvation in the aftermath of World War I, Save the Children expanded to include members in much of the developed and some of the developing world (with member representation in South America and South Asia as well as in Africa). Because of its strong presence in the developed world, it was not unusual to have multiple Save members active in any given country, often working without any coordination and in some instances with active rivalry and competition for human and financial resources.

To engage the challenge of continuing to develop local capacity while avoiding competitive duplication of efforts, Save the Children, with the initial leadership of the "Big Four" members (the United States, the United Kingdom, Norway, and Sweden), determined that it would establish a more centralized coordination of its global programs. The result has been a sometimes difficult negotiation of contractual agreements with members to institutionalize Save the Children International, headquartered in London. While the new structure promises to reduce the uncoordinated competition among its thirty members that are operating in some ninety countries, it also expects to achieve more focused support for enhancement of local operating strength in developing countries.

The IRC, World Vision, CARE, and Save the Children are all working hard to move historically Western organizations to focus on enhancing the capacity of developing countries to take increased responsibility for the advancement of local communities. The quite different trajectories of these four agencies demonstrate that there are no easy answers to the tough questions at stake. It is therefore worth looking at yet one more model, namely relief and development organizations based from their very origin in the developing world.

## A Developing Country as a Base for International Development

BRAC exemplifies this alternative model. The acronym initially stood for the "Bangladesh Rehabilitation Assistance Committee" and then was changed to the "Bangladesh Rural Advancement Committee." But since BRAC expanded first to urban areas in Bangladesh (in 1994) and then (beginning in 2002) to ten developing countries abroad, it has preferred to use the acronym alone.

While all five organizations share a commitment to enhancing local capacity, BRAC is different from the IRC, World Vision, CARE, and Save the Children in two fundamental ways. The first and probably the most striking is that BRAC is now and since its founding has been based in one of the poorest countries in the world. And the second—contradicting the expectations that the first difference might raise—is that BRAC generates over 70 percent of its revenue from its own operations.

BRAC traces its origins back to the founding of Bangladesh. When what is now Bangladesh fought for its independence from Pakistan, the founder of BRAC, Fazle Hasan Abed, was an accountant who worked for Shell Oil Ltd. The battle for independence dramatically changed his life. He left his position at Shell, moved to London, and worked to raise awareness and money for the struggle underway in what the world then knew as East Pakistan.

After the war, Abed returned to a newly independent Bangladesh to find his native country devastated. Not only was the economy in ruins, but millions of refugees who had fled to India during the war were returning and in need of assistance in reestablishing their lives and livelihoods. To respond to these dire challenges, Abed founded the Bangladesh Rehabilitation Assistance Committee (which is now, as I have noted, usually called just BRAC) to provide aid to returning refugees in remote areas of northeastern Bangladesh.

Abed, now Sir Fazle after the United Kingdom awarded him knighthood in 2010, has continued to lead BRAC since its founding. Together with his Bangladeshi leadership team, he has built BRAC into a remarkable engine of economic development in Bangladesh. As its effectiveness in its home country has become better known in the developed world, BRAC has also received grants for its work from private entities like the Gates Foundation, international agencies like UNICEF, and government ministries like the UK Department for International Development and Australia's AusAID. But most of its revenues (to repeat, over 70 percent) continue to be generated from its own initiatives—for example, in farming (including poultry, dairy, and tea), in local crafts, in microfinance, and in financial services.

While BRAC generates revenue from some of its enterprises, its focus is on overcoming poverty. Microfinance programs and financial services are designed to allow the poorest of the poor to begin to support themselves more adequately. So are efforts to improve farming and to generate revenue by moving locally produced foods and crafts cheaply and efficiently to markets. Along with this concern for income generation for its beneficiaries, BRAC is heavily engaged in helping to provide basic education and health services delivered by community-based health workers. These initiatives, too, are mostly funded by resources generated from BRAC's own activities, although now also supplemented by donor grants.

In recent years, while maintaining its base in Bangladesh, BRAC has, as I have noted in describing the evolution of its name, also established programs in other places. Not counting its affiliated offices (mostly dedicated to fundraising) in the United States and the United Kingdom, BRAC is now active in ten further countries, all in the developing world. Much of the grant money that BRAC receives is for projects that expand successful programs from Bangladesh into such countries as Afghanistan, Liberia, South Sudan, Uganda, and Sri Lanka.

In terms of numbers of employees (some 120,000) and beneficiaries affected (it claims 130 million), BRAC is arguably the largest nongovernmental relief and development organization in the world. Even in terms of financial expenditures, it is, at over $800 million, among the largest globally. Therefore, BRAC needs to be better known and more seriously considered as a model for enhancing global capacity. No doubt much depends on remarkable leadership at a critical inflection point in the history of its home country. Yet the focus on enabling the poorest of the poor to generate income by an agency that is itself grounded in a developing country suggests approaches that invite, if not replication, then at least further application.

## The Global Challenge of Enhancing Local Capacity

The IRC, World Vision, CARE, Save the Children, and BRAC are all engaged in enhancing local capacity around the world. Among shared efforts are recruiting, training, and promoting national staff; supporting health care and education to advance both this and the next generation; focusing attention in particular on the needs of women and girls; providing opportunities for income generation; and supporting the development of legal protection systems and good governance. The common ground across program areas suggests the merits of even more partnerships among the organizations and also the desirability of learning from each other as to best practices.

The remarkable achievements of BRAC, especially its adeptness in generating revenue from its economic development activities for investment into basic service delivery, focus attention on ways to build from the ground up in even the poorest regions. Furthermore, its rapid growth indicates that there are prospects for bringing poverty alleviation projects to scale without an unrealistic reliance on ever larger levels of aid from the developed world. While we must avoid the threat of turning BRAC into the latest bearer of missionary good news, we need to realize the promise of collective learning from its experience in Bangladesh over the past forty years.

Some lessons are clear from practices that are already shared. Relying as quickly and as extensively as is feasible on staff from affected communities is emphatically one. A second is that providing basic health care, including potable water and decent sanitary conditions, pays long-term dividends.

A third is that the protection and the legal and financial empowerment of women and girls bring big benefits to the entire community, as CARE in particular has emphasized.

One theme that cuts across all of those exemplary practices is education. While it is an area in which all these organizations work, it may be one in which outside partners can stimulate more collaboration. For example, in programs that already are emphasized, like primary and even preschool education, comparative assessment programs would help in highlighting best practices.

Even more, for needs on which less attention is focused—for example, advanced training and education for national staff—fresh opportunities would be welcome. Because it launched its own university a little over ten years ago (which now has about six thousand students), BRAC has special resources to offer. But each of the agencies discussed has partnerships with a variety of educational institutions that might be expanded to the others. In addition, there are specialized educational institutions that focus specifically on training for relief and development with the national staff of NGOs explicitly in view.

An imaginative and practice-based example is the Future Generations Graduate School. Founded by Daniel Taylor and accredited in the United States, its programs are specifically designed for staff of international relief and development organizations. Students continue in their positions, interacting with faculty and other students online. Over a two-year period they participate in four one-month residential sessions with faculty and fellow students. Each student also develops a two-year practicum for field-based research in his or her own community. There is limited financial aid, which together with some support from the student's organization makes the two-year program affordable. The degree earned is an M.A. in Applied Community Change. I can testify that IRC national staff members have enrolled in the program to great benefit.

I will adhere to my preliminary conclusion to refrain from proposing reforms for education, health care, and the tax code in the United States. I simply reaffirm that building local capacity is also a critically important priority for the United States and the rest of the developed world. As for the developing world, and even more so for the most impoverished countries that need a boost to get to the first rung of the development ladder, investing in the enhancing of local capacity must be at the top of the agenda.

Leading agencies like Save the Children, CARE, World Vision, and the IRC have pressed hard for this priority. BRAC embodies it in a most fundamental way. Now it is up to the rest of us to commit the resources required to help enhance the capacity of those who can and should and will work their own way out of abject poverty and in the process contribute to creating a more inclusive global society.

# 10   Religious Communities as a
Resource for Conflict Resolution

IT WOULD BE TOUGH to survey armed struggles around the world and not see religion as a significant variable in a large proportion of the dissension. Regrettably, religious commitment all too frequently serves as the trigger for antagonism, or at least accentuates the animosities that fuel the fighting. Yet despite this role in contributing to tension, religious beliefs and practices are potential resources for work toward conflict resolution. Especially if local capacity is developed on a global scale, there is the prospect that this potential may be more fully actualized. The result can and should be a determined move toward communities that include adherents of multiple traditions.

## Andrew Carnegie and Reinhold Niebuhr

Through my involvement with the Carnegie Council for Ethics in International Affairs, I have been reminded repeatedly of the devotion Andrew Carnegie had toward averting war and indeed to moving decisively toward world peace. Among the many philanthropic vehicles that Carnegie launched was the Church Peace Union. Established in 1914 shortly before the outbreak of World War I, it represents his deeply felt conviction that conflict could be contained—and that religious communities could contribute to that salutary outcome.

---

This chapter draws on remarks I offered in Sarajevo in June 2014 at a symposium to commemorate both the centennial of the founding of the Carnegie Council for Ethics in International Affairs and, paradoxically, the onset of the First World War.

From the beginning, the Church Peace Union was not as exclusively Christian as its name suggested. To take the most salient consideration in the American context, it included Jewish as well as Protestant and Catholic participants. Through their combined voices, the Union expressed the hope of its founder that religious communities could together generate energy and support for peace rather than war—a hope that was at the very least deferred when war broke out at virtually the moment of its establishment.

A generation later, as the West marched toward yet another major conflict, similar efforts were launched. As noted in chapter 7, in 1933 Albert Einstein proposed that a committee of notables be convened in New York City to work with counterparts in Europe in rescuing refugees from Nazi persecution. Among the leaders who responded to the call was Reinhold Niebuhr, the distinguished Lutheran theologian and ethicist who had come a few years earlier from his pastorate in Detroit to a professorship at the Union Theological Seminary in New York. Niebuhr chaired this committee from 1939–1941, as it renamed itself the International Rescue Committee.

In contrast to what could fairly be characterized as Carnegie's perhaps uncritical and certainly idealistic embrace of peace, Niebuhr represented a quite tough-minded realism on matters of international relations. Yet the institutions that these two quite different personalities represent have contributed in mutually reinforcing ways to the cause of conflict resolution. It may therefore be worth tracing the two lineages.

Carnegie's Church Peace Union has evolved over time, though perhaps more in name than in purpose. To call attention to its concern for global issues beyond the ecclesiastical concerns that its original name suggested, the Church Peace Union became the Council on Religion and International Affairs in 1961, then the Council on Ethics and International Affairs in 1986, and finally the Council for Ethics in International Affairs in 2005. Yet through this series of name changes, the Union or Council continued its concern for peace and international understanding—for example, as a staunch advocate for the League of Nations between the two world wars and for the United Nations after World War II. Its concern for conflict resolution has continued with an emphasis on the need for social justice.

It has also retained its founding intention of involving religion in international affairs.

Niebuhr's role in the International Rescue Committee was certainly not as central as Carnegie's had been in shaping the institutional purposes of the Church Peace Union and its successors. But at its best, the IRC has continued both Niebuhr's tough-minded realism in assessing international issues and his advocacy for compassionate responses to the needs that crises generate. In spite of—and in some respects because of—its origins in rescuing large numbers of Jewish refugees from Nazi persecution, the IRC has been resolutely nonsectarian. As is emphasized in chapter 9, it has, however, become deeply engaged in local communities around the world. As a result, there is the prospect that the IRC as well as the Carnegie Council may contribute to our sense of how and why religious communities are a crucial resource for conflict resolution worldwide.

## The Salience of Religion in Current Conflicts

In chapter 7, I sketched how the face of conflict today differs from the dominant pattern of war for the more than three centuries between the Peace of Westphalia in 1648 and the serial conflicts in Vietnam of the twentieth century. To repeat, the pattern for those more than three hundred years was engagement between nation-states or coalitions of nation-states, in contrast to the tendency both before and after that period. In that respect, it is worth remembering that the Peace of Westphalia represents the close of the Thirty Years' War, also known as the Wars of Religion. While few would call the conflicts today exclusively "wars of religion," differences of religious allegiance are certainly a salient dimension of much of the fighting.

It is hard to resist moving our thoughts immediately to the Middle East. While I will in due course focus on the multiple conflicts in that tumultuous region, I deem it important to note that the salience of religion is also evident in other places. So that we do not consider the Middle East as an anomalous instance based only on its historic role in generating Jewish, Christian, and Muslim traditions, we should see conflicts there in the context of broader patterns also evident in Asia and, perhaps to a lesser extent, in Africa and Latin America.

As I noted in chapter 2, my family lived in Kandy, Sri Lanka, for a year (from 1969 to 1970) to allow me to study Theravāda Buddhism. It was an idyllic year in a beautiful and welcoming place. To watch the downward spiral of Sri Lanka over the more than four intervening decades has therefore been even more dismaying than if my family and I had not had our wonderful time there. As an admirer and student of Buddhism, I have been ever more distressed to witness the aggressively hostile role that some Theravāda monks have played in fomenting sectarian hostility. There are, to be sure, underlying linguistic differences in that the language of the Buddhist majority is Sinhalese and of the Hindu minority is Tamil, with less clear linguistic divides in the smaller Christian and Muslim communities. But there can be no doubt that the aggressive stance of the Sinhalese majority against the Tamils has been reinforced through the support of Buddhist communities, including leading monks.

An even more recent instance of Theravāda Buddhist action that violates every tenet of the tradition's commitment to nonviolence is the attacks on Muslims in Myanmar. Here, too, Buddhist monks have been among the fomenters of ruthless assaults against defenseless Muslims. I first visited Burma in 1970, and I am all the more deeply chagrined to have witnessed in my most recent visit in 2012 the burned-out villages of Rohingya Muslims in Rakhine State.

Instances can be multiplied: attacks of Hindus on Muslims in India and retaliation of Muslims on Hindus; Muslim-Christian violence in Nigeria, Mali, and the Central African Republic; atrocities between Shia and Sunni Muslims in Pakistan; lingering tensions between Protestant and Catholic Christians in Northern Ireland; and many more. The question is not whether religion plays a role in such conflicts; it is all too clear that religious affiliation too often contributes to, exacerbates, or even animates some of the most ferocious hostilities. The question is rather whether there is any prospect that religious communities can also be a resource for conflict resolution.

## Syria as a Crucial Test Case

This question comes into sharp focus in current conflicts in what we in the West call the Middle East. The civil war in Syria has created the largest numbers of both internally displaced persons and refugees in decades. Out of a population of about twenty-two million, over seven million Syrians still within the country have had to flee their homes. Some three million more have fled into neighboring Lebanon, Jordan, Turkey, and Iraq. So the crisis is not only inside Syria but also throughout the region.

Certainly the civil war in Syria is not simply a battle between rival religious groups. The initial protests enlisted a broad cross-section of those dissatisfied with the long rule of Hafez al-Assad and the slow if not halted change promised by his son Bashar upon the latter's accession to the presidency. At first, concern was not centrally with religion, even though both Assads and most of their senior advisors and government officials were Alawites, a small sect of Shiite Muslims not widely accepted even among other Shiites outside of Syria and certainly not embraced by the majority Sunni community. Still, instead of focusing on religious differences, the call of the protesters was for more general reform and movement toward a more open and inclusive state.

But as the civil war has broadened in geographical scope, extended markedly in time, and intensified in violence, religious divisions have become more salient. The initial protesters included disenchanted Alawites and other Shiites as well as Sunnis and secularists. What became the initial rebellion therefore had the potential to forge a common agenda across the religious lines and also to include secular dissidents. Since Saudi Arabia and other Gulf states have provided aid and Sunni jihadist fighters, this kind of broad-based coalition has become less likely, though it almost certainly remains the only feasible foundation for a resolution to the conflict.

Here, neighboring Iraq offers a lesson on how not to proceed. However ill-advised the 2003 invasion of Iraq was, the overthrow of Saddam Hussein offered the opportunity to forge a broadly based government that included both Sunnis and Shia. The tough decisions would in any case have been how to include at least some representation of Ba'athist officials who were instrumental in keeping the government functional. The decision of the United States, as articulated by Paul Bremer in his role as administrator of the Coalition Provisional Authority, to force a complete "de-Ba'thification" of the Iraqi civil service in effect set the new Iraqi government on a path of total control by Shia forces. Since 2003, there have been sporadic efforts by both the United States and Iraqis to press for a more inclusive government. But under Prime Minister Nouri al-Malaki, the record became one of increasing Shia dominance and growing Sunni disenchantment—all the more serious since Sunnis represent at least a third and perhaps as much as 40 percent of the population.

In the volatile setting of a vicious civil war, Syria can and should rise to the occasion of forging an inclusive coalition as the core of the next government. The coalition will no doubt be built around the Sunni majority (both Arab and Kurd) of the population. But it must also include participation from the Shia minority, with at least some representation of the Alawites, the largest subgroup of Shia in Syria and the one with the controlling influence in the governments of both Hafez al-Assad and Bashar al-Assad.

In the past, Syria has had a proud history of allowing vibrant Christian churches and even a vigorous Jewish community to flourish. Even as recently as 2008, I had the privilege of visiting both Christian churches and a Jewish synagogue in Damascus, though by then most members of the Jewish community had already emigrated. While relatively few Christians and even fewer Jews remain, they and committed secularists who are open to participating should also be included in a broad-based coalition.

Those extremists who insist on an exclusively Sunni social order may well opt out of any such coalition, as no doubt will their jihadist allies from neighboring Sunni-controlled countries. Any such decisions will make ending the violence more challenging. Yet the goal must be to form a coalition of the willing from across the spectrum of religious and ethnic groups in Syria to allow the restoration of order and a functioning government.

Indispensable to achieving this outcome is the religious leadership, especially of the Sunni and of the Shia communities. While there is a considerable history of relatively amicable coexistence among the Shia and Sunni communities in Syria, it will be an enormous challenge to overcome the antipathies not only of past injustices but also of current ruthless bloodshed. Building on shared affirmations and respecting particular differences in belief and practice would and should allow for movement toward a coalition of the willing. It will certainly not be easy. But as the scene of the worst humanitarian disaster in a generation, Syria has a chance to move toward a positive outcome—and its religious communities have the opportunities to lead the way.

It is of course easy to point to the need for this leadership. There is certainly a long and arduous path to achieve such a broad-based participation in a coalition for inclusive government. But a first step in this path is to recognize that that there is no alternative route out from the prospect of decades of violence and chaos. While there will be other escapes proposed, a simple test can sort the ones with any chance of success from those doomed to failure: does the plan include at its core support from both Sunni and Shia communities? Unless it does, it is not viable—as Nouri al-Maliki has demonstrated in neighboring Iraq.

## The Contribution of International Religious Collaboration

Westerners are certainly not in a position to enlist Syrian religious leaders to seize the initiative in rallying their respective communities to power sharing and a peaceful outcome to the turmoil in which they are embroiled. But the quagmire in Syria is a classic case in which religion could serve as a resource for conflict resolution. The fact that religion is almost always—and often rightly—viewed as part of the problem rather than as a source for solutions should be a call to action on the part of religious traditions worldwide.

As occurred after World War I, there was at the close of World War II a surge of activity among religious leaders—especially in the West, but also in Asia—to press for establishing a durable global peace. Much of that energy focused initially on the United Nations. But it then also sought other outlets.

By the early 1960s, four American religious leaders determined that a global movement focused specifically on religion was required. The four were prominent Protestant, Catholic, and Jewish leaders: Maurice Eisendrath, executive director and president of the Union of American Hebrew Congregations; Dana McLean Greeley, Unitarian pastor and president of the Unitarian Universalist Association; John Wesley Lord, bishop in the Methodist Church; and John Wright, Roman Catholic bishop. Through their efforts and quite a few other initiatives—including several meetings in the United States and also a delegation of twenty Americans who undertook an international peace mission—the first gathering of what became the World Conference of Religion for Peace was held in Kyoto, Japan, in October 1970.

This meeting in Kyoto included discussions of disarmament, development, and human rights. It also led to the formal establishment of the World Conference of Religion for Peace (which became the World Conference on Religion and Peace in 1974 and is now known as Religions for Peace), with a board of directors and a headquarters located at the Church Center for the United Nations in New York. There were further world conferences in Louvain, Belgium (1974), in Princeton, New Jersey (1979), in Nairobi, Kenya (1984), and in Melbourne, Australia (1989). In addition, an effort was made to launch service programs—in particular, the Boat People Project in 1976–1977 and the Khmer Fund in 1979–1980.

Despite the interest in also developing practical programs, the thrust of these conferences was at the policy level to encourage engagement by religious communities in pressing for world peace. As a participant in the 1984 conference in Nairobi, I can testify to this focus on generating religious collaboration in the cause of peace around the globe. But while this goal is surely a worthy aspiration, it is not adequate alone to meeting crises like the current disaster in Syria. Instead, we are faced with the imperative of also seeking to support local efforts that enlist partners on the ground. In acknowledging this imperative, international initiatives to enlist religion in the cause of conflict resolution in effect are recognizing the need to follow the same path as international relief and development organizations. The challenge is indeed to build local capacity globally.

## The Challenge of Supporting Local Initiatives

My description of the National Solidarity Program in chapter 7 and all of the issues explored in chapter 9 stress how critical it is to build the capacity of local partners and staff recruited locally. If there is to be any hope of enlisting religion as a resource for conflict resolution, the process must include—and probably begin with—people on the ground where the battles are underway. How to pursue this objective is not at all clear and in any case extremely difficult, but pursuing it needs to be a top priority if religious communities are to be a resource for reducing rather than contributing to intensifying conflict.

One approach moves from international connections to the regional and local level. Already established contacts through international relationships seek to identify counterparts in regional and local units of their own traditions and to enlist those counterparts in interacting with colleagues in other communities. The meetings of Religions for Peace (and its predecessors under slightly different names) illustrate the beginnings of this process insofar as they establish networks that cut across traditions and also across divisions within nominally unified traditions. Similarly promising are the Global Ethics Fellows and the Ethics Fellows for the Future, recent initiatives of the Carnegie Council for Ethics in International Affairs.

Yet such networks remain at a quite elevated level (even in the case of the younger generation of fellows for the future) in the traditions represented, and in terms of geography are heavily tilted toward the United States, Europe, and Asia, with a notable underrepresentation from Africa and the Middle East. Furthermore, in regard to religious diversity, Islam in all its varieties is not as fully represented as it needs to be. In view of the demographics of current conflicts worldwide, existing global networks of religious leaders and institutions must therefore be broadened and deepened to overcome their limited reach where it is most needed.

One small organization that seeks to bridge the divide between Western nongovernmental organizations and local religious leadership is the Tanenbaum Center for Interreligious Understanding, founded by Georgette Bennett and headquartered in New York City. It has a program, called "Peacemakers in Action: Profiles of Religion in Conflict Resolution," which aims to enlist local leaders of religious communities in mediating between opposing sides to resolve conflicts that include a religious dimension. The roster of peacemakers is, moreover, reflective of where current conflicts are underway, notably the Middle East, Africa, and such countries in Asia and Latin America as Afghanistan, Pakistan, Sri Lanka, El Salvador, and Colombia. Also included on the roster of peacemakers are representatives of immediately post-conflict countries like Bosnia and Herzegovina, Kosovo, and Ireland. In regular workshops these peacemakers have the opportunity to learn from each other—and to teach those others of us who have the opportunity to participate.

What is required is both to focus the attention of global networks devoted to interreligious understanding and collaboration on conflict areas and to scale up the activities of the few organizations like the Tanenbaum Center that are already concentrating on this concern. The result would in effect complement the efforts of global networks to enlist their local counterparts with a second approach that seeks to work more directly at the local level. Here the track record of international relief and development organizations in building local capacity not only is a model to be emulated but also provides the promise of potential partners. Yet here too there are many pitfalls. Even when a nongovernmental organization is most emphatically grounded in local communities, the connection to religious authorities is not always easy or straightforward.

I call attention again to the example of BRAC, which I described in chapter 9. Even though BRAC is directly at work in well over half of Bangladesh's villages with programs that address the needs of the poorest residents, its efforts have not been without tensions in relating to religious authorities and even individuals or groups of devotees. In particular, BRAC's commitment to foster the interests of women and girls has on occasion elicited protests from traditional Muslims. Recent examples include disputes about whether or not wearing the niqab fits the dress code at BRAC University and about a series of posters that question whether such practices as "verbal divorce" are acceptable. But despite heated criticism, BRAC's involvement in thousands of villages to address the needs of the poor has opened opportunities for understanding—in this case, less among opposed religious communities than between divergent interpretations within Muslim communities and also between Islamic and secular viewpoints. The challenge is to work with religious communities to press forward through this opening.

The International Rescue Committee has an educational program called "Healing Classrooms." Because we work in many places in response to emergencies caused by conflict, we conduct this program in more than twenty countries. The curriculum is designed to help children—from those of preschool age to adolescents—deal with the trauma of the conflict that they have endured. It is an excellent example of helping victims come to terms with the antagonisms they have encountered. But in large part because the IRC is a nonsectarian organization and attracts staff who affirm that orientation, our Healing Classrooms program has been reluctant to engage religious differences directly, even in places like the Palestinian Territories, where ethnic and religious tensions and attendant stereotypes are all but unavoidable.

The IRC and other non-faith-based organizations need to overcome their collective reluctance to engage religious differences directly. Ironically, even Western faith-based organizations like World Vision have a special difficulty in engaging the role of religious adherence in generating conflict. A deliberate policy of not allowing proselytization can all too easily result in treating religious differences as topics also not to be addressed. Yet nonsectarian and faith-based organizations alike can and should enlist their well-earned credibility with local actors to press for coalitions that cut across sectarian divides.

Such examples of challenges at the local level, as well as the need for larger-scale and increased inclusiveness in international networks, demonstrate that there is a long way to go before religious communities become more a resource for reducing rather than a source for increasing antagonism. But the examples also demonstrate the potential for greater understanding at the local level. The challenge is to build on that local potential even while developing larger, more inclusive, and more representative international networks so that religious communities can indeed become a resource for the mitigation of violence and even for conflict resolution.

## The Need for Examples Also in the Developed World

As crucial as it is for local religious leaders in tension-filled regions to engage in the work of reconciliation, it is also important for counterparts in more peaceful and wealthier countries to provide support for initiatives on the ground in war zones. Here too there is an enormous gap between aspirations and achievements. One contribution beyond financial assistance can and should be to offer an example of more or less peaceful coexistence in the face of deep disagreement—whether across ethnic, political, or religious divisions. But even that limited contribution is hard to deliver. Still more problematic is the fact that any such offering from the West will be deemed yet one more neocolonial attempt to dictate norms.

Despite such all-but-certain criticisms, it is worth considering examples of the few instances that have worked in the West. The common, most immediate critical reaction from the developing world is that in the secular West, with its focus on individual autonomy, there is no space for seriously engaged religious commitment. In much of Western Europe it is certainly arguable that such tolerance as there is for multiple religious views is the result of indifference to all of them. That may be an unfair characterization because it seems to rule out value-based and community-grounded commitments, whether in established churches, dissident religious groups, or non-religiously affiliated communities. Yet as a first approximation as to the ethos of Europe as a whole, it is not unfair to conclude that secular individualism trumps religious devotion for much of the population.

The United States offers a less clear target for the charge that there is no space for religiously serious commitment. Ironically, the recent higher profile of Christian-affiliated conservatives might suggest to outsiders that the United States is just one more example of a country that allows one religious tradition to dominate the broader society to the point of excluding all other traditions. While the threat of this exclusion of other positions cannot casually be dismissed, there is in fact a long history of rejecting such exclusivism. The issue is how the insistence on allowing multiple positions is construed. Is it only that each individual is free to form his or her own beliefs and practices? Or is there also freedom for multiple religious communities to express their commitments?

Most Americans would answer in the affirmative not only to individual liberty in taking religious positions but also to the freedom of religious communities to express their commitments. There may be, to quote Thomas Jefferson's phrasing, a wall of separation between church and state, but that wall allows full expression of religious convictions on the part of multiple religious communities. The key requirement is that government may not control religion, even if religious convictions unavoidably shape the ways that adherents participate in public life.

The result is that members of multiple religious communities unavoidably participate together in shaping public policy. Viewed globally, this outcome is remarkably rare. It is, moreover, what countries beset by strife that is in part based on religious differences need to achieve: coalitions, or at least agreements as to sharing power among sharply divided parties, that allow the basic order required for nonviolent social interactions.

The deficiencies in the American political process are glaringly visible. Included are the indefensibly influential role of large private financial contributions in shaping elections and the all-but-stalled legislative process in Washington, D.C. It is therefore heartening that, at least on this set of issues, the United States has experience that may be of service elsewhere: a set of arrangements that in principle allow adherents of differing and often opposed religious beliefs and practices to participate fully in a shared polity.

How similar arrangements can be codified and institutionalized in various social settings is, to be sure, a big challenge of design and implementation. In the long run, both the society as a whole and the local religious communities must address this challenge together. But even if that process is demanding, the alternative to starting it forthwith is continued antagonism and conflict.

# 11    Religion and Ecology

THE DIRE NEED for inclusive communities is inescapable in conflict situations worldwide, but it is in the end also unavoidable in the most encompassing challenge that confronts the human community—namely, the ecological threat to the viability of life on earth. Because this challenge confronts the human race as a whole, it must be engaged globally. To respond in ways that offer any prospect of success will require that we marshal all of the resources of our intellectual capacities and our multiple cultural and religious traditions.

## Religion, Modern Secular Culture, and Ecology

We are all in this ecological crisis together. It may be self-evident but it is still worth repeating: this crisis confronts everyone in that it threatens the very viability of life on Earth, and therefore requires responses that will affect us all. This sense of being in a crisis together is vividly captured in images of the Earth photographed from space—images that are in danger of becoming shopworn but that still express a profound truth. All of us, including our various religious and cultural traditions, have contributed to the gravity of the threat we face.

Almost sixty years ago, Lynn White wrote an arresting essay entitled "The Historical Roots of our Ecologic Crisis," which was published in *Science* in 1967 and has received widespread attention over the years from

---

This chapter is a revised version of "Religion, Modern Secular Culture, and Ecology," *Daedalus* 130, no. 4 (Fall 2001): 23–30.

scientists as well as humanists. It is worth returning to his article because it continues to be instructive, not only through its telling insights, but also through its equally revealing omissions. White correctly identifies the dominant strain or core structure of Western theism that represents God as transcending the world and humanity as exercising dominion over the natural order. Where he falls short is in his failure to notice how other elements in the structure of biblical religion in effect counterbalance the invitation to exercise human sovereignty over nature. Two such elements are crucial: the affirmation of creation as the handiwork of God and therefore as good, and the record of humanity's fall and consequent need for redemption.

That nature is God's creation and therefore good calls for respectful care and stewardship. White is aware of what he terms "an alternative Christian view," which he delineates almost exclusively in reference to St. Francis of Assisi. But he does not interpret the theme of care and stewardship for the divine creation as a central element in the structure of Jewish and Christian religion—and also of Islam, though White does not include Muslim religion in his purview.

Similarly crucial for counterbalancing the motif of human sovereignty over nature is the biblical story of fall and redemption. The destiny of the faithful is after all not to be realized in worldly rulership. Especially in much of Christian piety, the human vocation is to be a pilgrim who is only passing through the fallen world and who must therefore tread lightly over the earth on the way to redemption in heaven.

This otherworldly orientation can of course cut both ways. It may lead to a disengagement that is, paradoxically, friendly to the environment from which it is estranged. But it may also result in the exploitation of the fallen world precisely because it is viewed as lacking intrinsic value. Thus even very traditional Western religious worldviews have a deeply equivocal relationship to our ecological crisis.

What is noteworthy, though, is that the force of the structural elements outlined by White becomes only more pronounced as increasing numbers of people find the traditional narrative of fall and redemption less and less compelling. If salvation in heaven is not the central goal of human life, then the prospect of sovereignty over the natural world takes on greater urgency. And if the evident evil in worldly affairs is to be overcome apart from any redemptive divine action, then vigorous human effort will be required.

Similarly, if God as creator is believed to have established a general order to nature but is no longer thought to intervene in particular events, then human will and intelligence can seek to understand and in time even attempt to control the natural world. Furthermore, if even the limited role attributed to this remote deity is no longer attractive or persuasive, then human effort is all the more crucial. Thus the rise of science and the correlative retreat of traditional theism from at least the late seventeenth century onward accentuated precisely the anthropocentric elements that White identifies as characteristic of Jewish and Christian religion.

To put the point bluntly, it is only as the transcendent God of biblical religion is no longer thought to intervene in the world either as creator or as redeemer that the full force of claims for human dominion over nature becomes evident.

In the twentieth century, this unrestrained human self-assertion over nature reached what remains its starkest expression in the literary and philosophical movement called existentialism. Like most broad cultural trends, existentialism has many variants that certainly do not agree in all their details. But the early thought of Martin Heidegger exerted enormous influence on the movement as a whole and in many respects illustrates its central tendencies. For Heidegger, the human self is, to use his language, "thrown" into an indifferent universe from which it must seize and shape whatever meaning can be attained. There is no created order to discover, nor is there any redemptive community. Instead the self-reliant individual must establish authentic existence in stark opposition both to nature and to the mores of any and all forms of social life—in particular, of the mass culture of modern society.

Existentialism offers a convenient depiction of both the glory and the travail of modern Western individualism. Its summons to authenticity, to self-actualization over against a conformist society and an indifferent nature, resonates with the energy, initiative, and independence of our most individualistic traditions. But existentialism also exemplifies the willful self-assertion and arrogance that all too frequently characterize Western attitudes both toward nature and toward the cultures of others.

There are of course substantial cultural resources for enriching this environmentally inhospitable and religiously impoverished individualism. Especially noteworthy are the contributions from a remarkable range of Asian traditions—from Hindu, Buddhist, Taoist, Shinto, and Confucian thought and practice. But the variety in the views expressed in those traditions registers powerfully how diverse each community is, how disparate their historical impacts have been, and how untenable it is to present any single tradition in self-congratulatory terms as consistently and effectively unified in its ecological orientation.

The result is that neither Asian traditions, nor the relatively fewer environmentally friendly themes of Jewish, Christian, and Muslim action and reflection, nor the orientations of indigenous communities in Africa, Oceania, and the Americas are by themselves adequate for addressing the environmental challenges we face. We cannot pick and emphasize only environmentally friendly motifs from multiple traditions. Nor can we simply embrace a unified position that affirms the whole of reality just as it is. Instead we must grapple with the fact that modern Western individualism and its institutional expressions in social, political, and economic life have become major historical forces across virtually all cultures—forces that we cannot ignore or wish away but rather must engage and incorporate into an ecologically responsible stance appropriate to the centuries ahead.

## Ecology and Inquiry in the University

One of the settings in which we can, should, and must grapple with this ecological crisis is our universities. It is scarcely surprising, in view of the history of their development, that modern research universities exemplify an advanced form of the very individualism that we must overcome. This exemplification is not only that individual members of at least Western academic institutions are in their personal styles highly individualistic, though that is certainly often true. It is also that, in developing academic disciplines as central to the organization of domains of knowledge, universities exhibit a pattern that parallels the role of individualism in the broader society.

Disciplinary specialization is a significant achievement of the research university. It has been remarkably effective in generating both understanding of specific data and general explanatory hypotheses. But this attainment of analytical rigor has as its correlate a depth of specialization that renders connections with other disciplinary approaches difficult at a time when we are becoming increasingly aware that many challenging intellectual problems, certainly including issues at the heart of our ecological crisis, do not fall neatly within the domain of a single discipline.

This state of affairs has predictably led to calls for interdisciplinary investigation. While completely understandable, such calls are problematic in ways that parallel the invocation of one or another religious or cultural tradition as the answer to our ecological crisis. Just as we cannot simply return to a state of innocence that antedates the historical emergence of modern Western individualism, so we cannot embrace a synthetic interdisciplinary approach that fails to incorporate the analytic strengths and achievements of disciplinary specialization.

What is required is therefore not interdisciplinary study, but rather multidisciplinary investigation comparable in rigor and depth to specialized research within a single discipline. With respect to the ecological crisis confronting us, one initiative is worth special attention because it seeks to enlist academic strengths from across the entire range of academic disciplines within the university—indeed, also from partner institutions—to address the challenges we must engage together. That initiative is the Columbia Earth Institute.

The heart of the Earth Institute is Columbia University's Lamont-Doherty Earth Observatory (LDEO). At LDEO, located on the Palisades overlooking the Hudson River, two hundred scientists from a remarkable array of disciplines and three hundred technical and support staff members conduct research across a wide range of projects devoted to understanding the earth as a complex set of interacting systems. Lamont scientists were the first to establish the theory of plate tectonics, produced the first mathematical models for accurately predicting El Niños, and first discovered that the core of the earth rotates at a rate different from that of the surface. The Lamont-Doherty Earth Observatory also for many years deployed the *Maurice Ewing*, a two-thousand-ton research vessel that gathers data around the world, and for a number of years also managed the Biosphere 2 in Oracle, Arizona. This massive constellation of efforts is designed to bring the most rigorous and disciplined research to bear on understanding the changing face of the earth, including such pressing challenges as global warming.

Joining forces with LDEO to constitute the Earth Institute are research efforts in the following entities within Columbia: the Department of Earth and Environmental Sciences, the School of International and Public Affairs, the Business School, the Law School, the Fu Foundation School of Engineering and Applied Science, and the Mailman School of Public Health. Combining multidisciplinary investigation with a multi-institutional structure is the Center for Environmental Research and Conservation (CERC), a consortium that draws together anthropologists, biologists, and policy analysts at Columbia with colleagues from the Black Rock Forest, the Wildlife Conservation Society (also known as the Bronx Zoo), the Wildlife Preservation Trust International, and the American Museum of Natural History. Other such multi-institution partnerships include shared research initiatives with the Laboratory of Populations at Rockefeller University, more than thirty years of collaboration with NASA's Goddard Institute for Space Studies, and the formation of the International Research Institute for Climate Prediction, a joint venture with the Scripps Institute of Oceanography that receives substantial federal government support through the National Oceanic and Atmospheric Administration (NOAA).

This cursory survey of the components of the Columbia Earth Institute can at most provide a general sense of the intensity and scope of the multidisciplinary investigation and multi-institutional collaboration that this complex set of initiatives exemplifies. While many of the individual and institutional contributions to this common effort have a long and distinguished history of involvement in environmental issues, the Earth Institute itself is still a very young organization. Therefore, it has not yet fully established itself and certainly has not fundamentally altered our approaches to environmental issues. But it represents those multidisciplinary and multi-institutional initiatives that will be indispensable for adequately grasping ecological challenges and then also turning inquiry into action.

## From Inquiry to Action

In ordering our inquiry so that it makes a difference in our collective action, universities and collaborators in other cultural institutions can contribute on two crucial fronts. The first is to understand and to demonstrate in compelling ways how current platforms of advanced industrial societies are not sustainable indefinitely, or even for very long. The second is to participate in developing alternative technical approaches and economic incentives that allow and encourage a break from unsustainable current practices.

To move forward on both fronts clearly requires joint efforts on the part of scientists and engineers on the one hand and policy professionals on the other. That such joint efforts are being launched is promising. But the interests that favor the continuation of current patterns of consumption are extremely powerful. Consequently, any campaign to conserve our environment must be solidly based on compelling scientific evidence and cogently expressed in terms of economic incentives and policy requirements.

Along with marshaling scientific, technical, and policy capabilities for addressing ecological issues, we must also enlist the full range of the world's cultural resources. The most significant initial outcome of such multicultural efforts may well be the demonstration that easy answers are inadequate. The representation of multiple voices from a rich variety of communities initially serves to demonstrate the extent of pluralism not only among traditions but also within each of them. Effective collaboration across traditions therefore entails greater complexity than has often been supposed but, paradoxically, may also be more readily attained, at least in partial and stepwise fashion.

Pluralism within traditions also testifies to the capacity for change in what remains a continuous line of development. Thus even the communities most inclined to invoke authoritative figures or texts in fact regularly take into account new data and respond creatively to the demands of novel situations. This capacity for change opens up opportunities for collaboration across traditions as minor or even submerged motifs in one community gain a higher profile through interaction with other communities in which those motifs are more prominent.

To take a critical instance, in seeking to counter the Western tendency toward unrestrained individualism, a major resource is the insistence of many religious and cultural traditions that humans in the end are parts of a larger whole to which their personal interests and ambitions are subordinate. In Western religious and cultural traditions, this holistic affirmation has not yet been a dominant theme insofar as God has been construed as outside the world; it has been muted still more as the divine has been relegated to the margins of natural life and human affairs. But even in Western traditions, there is a persistent testimony that God is intimately involved with the world and indeed incorporates the world into the divine life.

This testimony is not confined to Francis of Assisi and a few other revolutionary figures, as Lynn White suggests when he refers to "an alternative Christian view." Instead it is a recurrent even if not dominant motif in the Bible and in Western theology and philosophy. Space does not allow a full elaboration of this claim; so a few illustrations will have to suffice.

Psalm 139 speaks for much Jewish and Christian piety:

> Where can I go from your spirit?
>     Or where can I flee from your presence?
> If I ascend to heaven, you are there;
>     if I make my bed in Sheol, you are there.
> If I take the wings of the morning
>     and settle at the farthest limits of the sea,
> even there your hand shall lead me,
>     and your right hand shall hold me fast.

If I say, "Surely darkness shall cover me,
　　and the light around me become night,"
even the darkness is not dark to you;
　　the night is as bright as the day,
　　for darkness is as light to you.
(Psalms 139:7–12)

For Christian theology, the central teaching of the incarnation affirms that the divine is integrally related to the human: a deity who is distant cannot be the God who loves and embraces the world in Christ.

As with traditional Jewish and Christian piety and reflection, modern secular appropriations of Western religion also illustrate the persistence of this holistic affirmation. Spinoza and Hegel are probably the most influential examples of Western philosophers who sought to restate the truths of Jewish and Christian religion in secular terms after the erosion of belief in a God outside the world. But instead of retreating to the remote God of Deism, Spinoza and Hegel insisted, each in his own way, that any coherent conception of God must include all of reality in the divine.

This holistic strain in Western traditions may attract attention out of proportion to its historical prominence in the context of interaction among religious traditions, especially once that interaction has moved beyond self-congratulatory representation to a seeking for common ground. This seeking of common ground does not imply an attempt to find a least common denominator to which various religious traditions can be reduced. Instead, the aim is to enrich and develop further the resources in each community for resisting unrestrained individualism through the affirmation of an inclusive reality into which personal interests and ambitions must be integrated.

We in the West have much to learn from religious and cultural traditions that locate the human within nature and that do not authorize the exploitation of nature to serve narrow human interests. At the same time, all of us as humans now confront ecological challenges that require vigorous effort to redirect the environmental impact of our species. Consequently, the energy and imagination that have contributed to the threats we face may also be a major resource for countering those very threats.

In this respect modern Western individualism, in both its secular and its religious expressions, may play a constructive role in ongoing deliberations on religion and ecology. While the recognition that the human is integral to a larger whole is crucial for cultivating an ecological ethos, this insight alone is not enough. In particular, this holistic affirmation of all that is does not directly address the important ethical question of how a more equitable sharing of limited resources may be attained.

Here again, each tradition can bring impressive resources to bear. But along with counterparts from other traditions, Western religious and secular perspectives certainly can and should play a role in the common cause of restoring ecological balance while also advancing toward a more equitable sharing of the Earth's scarce resources. Only this joining of environmental concern with a commitment to justice is worthy of the best in each of our diverse traditions.

To integrate an ethos of care for the earth as our common home with an ethic that engages the issues of equity is, I submit, the optimal outcome for serious reflection on the interrelationship of ecology and religion. We certainly have not yet achieved this integration. But this unity is the reality we affirm even as we work together to realize it.

Engaging the ecological threat to the viability of human life on Earth is integral to the challenge of realizing inclusive communities. As an imperative that cuts across cultural and religious traditions and demands contributions from all social strata and intellectual disciplines, it is well situated to focus the attention called for and enlist the efforts required. Our ecosystem is in fact the most inclusive of the communities that we share as fellow denizens of the earth, and we must therefore collaborate in caring for this common home, even if we do not agree as to whether it is also integral to an even more encompassing reality that inspires our awe and invites our worship.

# 12    Why Community?

IN THIS CHAPTER, I would like to reinforce the core argument first advanced in my introduction and then illustrated in diverse situations throughout the intervening chapters. The book as a whole is in effect a mosaic: it expresses common motifs represented in a variety of settings. As I noted at the outset, my hope is that an emphasis on recurrent themes strengthens the overall case.

In keeping with that approach, this chapter provides a summary of the central issues and includes contemporary examples to illustrate the remarkable range of the ramifications of those issues. At a time when all social ideologies have become suspect, Western individualism represents an alternative with significant appeal to educated elites, but it also elicits strong resistance in traditional societies. My core argument is that to address the dimension of this resistance that is warranted, the values of individualism can and should be integrated into an affirmation of community.

## Beyond Totalitarianism and Individualism

With the collapse of the Soviet Union, the last decade of the twentieth century saw the demise of state-controlled totalitarian ideology as a viable public posture for governments. Countries as diverse as China, North Korea, Myanmar, Sudan, Zimbabwe, Saudi Arabia, Iran, and Kazakhstan illustrate the multiple variants of totalitarianism that continue to domi-

---

This chapter includes some material that initially appeared under the title "Dreams, Dreads, and the New Global Community" in *Reflections* 99, no. 2 (Fall 2012), 38–45.

nate substantial populations. But the leadership of all of these countries is, like Russia itself, seeking ways to project a national identity that breaks with totalitarianism.

This collapse of state-controlled totalitarianism as a viable ideology in the first instance does seem to enhance the appeal of Western individualism, in particular among educated strata of a considerable range of societies. In the countries formed out of the former Soviet Union, certainly including Russia, there has been public (even if often deliberately ineffective) support for democratic processes that provide protection for individual freedom of expression and action. Similarly, there is resistance to totalitarian control—and advocacy for greater openness to multiple positions—in countries ranging (to take a sampling in alphabetical order) from Brazil and China to Iran, Myanmar, Tunisia, Uganda, Ukraine, and Zimbabwe.

Yet resistance to totalitarian ideologies does not translate simply and directly into support for Western individualism. Indeed, such resistance may include a forthright rejection of what are deemed the excesses of individualism. Those excesses are resisted with special vehemence when their advocates presume that the individualism developed in the modern West takes priority over other cultural traditions.

## Individuals and Communities

As I have maintained multiple times in previous chapters, the various forms of individualism that have developed in the Enlightenment and post-Enlightenment West are themselves social and cultural products of quite particular traditions. While such traditions may well aspire to be universally relevant or even universally compelling, they are nonetheless grounded in specific places and times. A self-aware individualism must therefore take into account the particular communities that shape its history and identity rather than assume as a given the individual conceived in abstraction from such communities.

It bears repeating that this imperative is especially compelling in the case of interaction with relatively traditional communities that view themselves as under assault from Western culture. These communities do not consider the tendencies they resist as culturally neutral perspectives but rather as ideologically antagonistic forces. The individualism that is integral to this alternative to traditional communities is correctly recognized as embedded in its own set of social and cultural patterns.

As I have previously noted in describing the resistance of traditional communities to Western individualism, the issues involved are not only conceptual but also institutional. For much of the West, individuals are viewed as relating to each other, beyond their immediate families, through relatively impersonal structures, particularly through market mechanisms, bureaucracies, and electronic and other media. In contrast, traditional communities have many more personal interactions: extended families, informal alliances, small-scale cooperatives, village elders, and religious authorities.

Connecting the individual to the larger society directly through markets, bureaucracies, or the media circumvents a whole network of intermediate institutions, beginning at the level of local communities. Thus institutional patterns taken for granted in the modern West in effect call into question the authority and even the viability of traditional relationships. Not surprisingly, this undermining of long-established practices elicits resistance in traditional societies.

Traditional communities are vividly aware of what is lost if individuals relate to each other only or primarily through impersonal mechanisms. But there are losses as well for more developed societies. The challenge is to acknowledge local and highly particular communities even as more inclusive ones—up to and embracing those that aspire to be universal—are not precluded and may even be affirmed.

## Religious Traditions as a Resource

As I have argued repeatedly—most extensively in the introduction and in chapter 5—a substantial resource for meeting this challenge of incorporating particular communities into more inclusive ones is the wealth of global human experience represented in religious affirmations, a resource that I venture to summarize again across several religious faiths because it represents the shared wisdom of thousands of years.

Among the most direct in focusing on human connection as the way to final truth are Chinese and Jewish traditions. For the Confucian, there is no access to the ultimate except through social relationships. Similarly, the dominant pattern of Jewish commitment has been to stress the communal character of relationship to the divine.

Among the vast diversity of Hindu traditions is a recurrent affirmation that *ātman* is *brahman*, that the self is one with the ultimate. This affirmation is also crucial in the history of Indian philosophy. But despite this identification of the self with the ultimate, the prevailing Indian pattern is to build on community solidarity as the foundation for any individual attainment.

Although it in the end became a complex of traditions differentiated from its Hindu origins, Buddhism exhibits the same pattern in and through its myriad forms. The earliest Buddhist traditions flatly deny that there is a self at all: over against the Hindu affirmation of *ātman* is an insistence on *anātman*, not self. In later developments, this insistence that there is no self becomes an acceptance of *śūnyatā*, the emptiness of all reality. Yet Buddhists too embrace the communities through which individuals advance, beginning with the *sangha*, the order of monks that became the bearer of Buddhist traditions.

There is a remarkably similar tendency across the range of Christian churches. Roman Catholics may insistently affirm institutional and even mystical bodies more encompassing than individuals, Orthodox Christians may nurture a sense of connection to the cosmos as a whole, and Protestants may focus on discrete selves. Yet all Christians affirm the crucial role of faithful communities in mediating the incorporation of the human into the divine, which for many Christians is also a community.

Islam offers an instance that is especially apt in view of the fact that so much of the most forceful resistance to Western secular individualism today is anchored in Muslim conviction. Islam too incorporates enormous diversity, as is evident in the often violent disagreements among divergent strains of Muslim tradition. While Islam has its mystics who claim direct communion with the ultimate—with Allah—for virtually all Muslims, the role of the community is still indispensable to their faith. In repudiating Western liberalism, advocates of Islam are rejecting what they deem to be a corrosive individualism that undermines this essential role of the community.

## The Challenge for a Conflicted World

As preceding chapters have described, the consumer society and mass culture of the West have the effect of extracting the individual from the communities that religious traditions affirm. Indeed, in its most recent and increasingly prevalent form, this Western individualism counters the connections of particular communities not only through markets, bureaucracies, and the media but also through Web-enabled relationships mediated through the Internet. Yet this secular, reductionist, Web-enabled individualism is in the end dependent on particular communities. In some cases this dependence is recognized. It may even be embraced with a yearning for the sense of connection and affirmation that has been lost. But it is crucial to affirm this impulse toward community while also remaining committed to the values of individualism.

This affirmation of both the individual and the community has a rich history at least as a theoretical proposition in both secular and religious contexts in the West as well as in other traditions. To embrace the values of individualism requires that a community allow criticism of its own ideals and practices. Indeed, it may even entail considering the inclusion of members from other traditions.

In practice, communities that are both self-critical and inclusive are admittedly rare in human experience. Furthermore, opposition to this position comes not only from the direction of uncritical and exclusionist traditionalists. Instead, any affirmation of community, even if it is self-critical and potentially inclusive, must also contend with precisely the individualism that has characterized much of Western social and cultural history since the Enlightenment.

It is therefore worth exploring cases in which this combination is, if not achieved, at least envisioned as a worthy goal. To buttress the argument that the combination, while rare, is not so exceptional as to be marginal, I will adduce as illustrations five quite different examples from disparate contemporary contexts that range from the quite familiar to the more exotic. First, in the West there continue to be civil society organizations that seek to integrate the activities of their individual members into larger social, economic, and political processes. Especially in the United States and the United Kingdom, such organizations carry on a deeply rooted tradition of voluntary associations, even as that tradition confronts a prevailing culture of unqualified individualism. The interaction among the societies that compose the self-proclaimed "European community" offers a second instance of the crosscurrents involved, as is evident in the tension between the larger body and more particular communities, especially at times of economic stress. Third, in societies as different from each other as the former Soviet Union, China, France, and Turkey, powerful secular states face either an already established or an emerging civil society as well as a host of traditional communities. Fourth, Iraq and Syria offer examples of similar crosscurrents, albeit without a long-established tradition of secularism as a basis for intercommunal order. Finally, in myriad local conflicts across the developing worlds, tribal, ethnic, and religious loyalties counter attempts to establish security and social order.

## The Anglo-American Tradition of Voluntary Associations

A pattern of voluntary associations offers rich resources for communitarian impulses in Anglo-American traditions. The term "voluntary association" itself implies individual volition: choosing to associate with one organization as distinguished from others. The very conception of voluntary associations therefore already suggests an individualism qualified by community, or a sense of association that moves beyond unquestioned belonging to a tribe.

Examples of voluntary associations are evident at every level of society, especially in the United States. Perhaps the most pervasive are the religious bodies that place a premium on a specific decision to join, as in Evangelical Christian churches. Civic associations of all kinds similarly illustrate voluntary membership: civic clubs (Rotary, Kiwanis, Lions, etc.); activities groups (crafts, hiking, and so on); political parties; and other membership organizations (Boy and Girl Scouts, labor unions, the National Rifle Association, AARP, the American Automobile Association, and the like).

The recent explosion of interest in Internet-based social networking takes the conception of voluntary association to a new level in terms of reach, a level in which virtual communities may paradoxically undermine physical ones. The correlations are complex and certainly do not imply direct causality. Indeed, many in-person voluntary associations have been in decline for decades, as is documented and popularized in writings like Robert D. Putnam's *Bowling Alone: The Collapse and Rise of American Community* (2000). In this sense the Internet is the latest example of a series of technology-based innovations that allow and even encourage individuals to relate to each other through various media rather than through in-person communities. Yet even in their virtual form, voluntary associations may afford resources for developing communities that are self-critical and inclusive, as is evident in dissident movements across a range of authoritarian societies, in particular in the Middle East.

## The European Union as a Political Example

The crosscurrents between particular communities and more inclusive associations are inescapable in the political project of forging a union among European states. Even within individual countries, there are of course tensions between local traditions and national goals—at times, as in the case of Belgium, tensions that extend to multiple languages. Such tensions become all the more pronounced when entire countries, with their different languages and national identities, seek to form economic and at least partial political unions.

Current financial pressures reveal how precarious the project is. While there is a single currency for most of the EU, there is no common fiscal policy, no shared financial regulation, no unified labor market, and no agreed-upon set of social benefits. Unsurprisingly, the result is a situation ripe for acrimony and resentment that strains whatever social bonds have developed over the six decades since the formation of the European Coal and Steel Community, the EU's precursor.

The EU demonstrates how powerful the centrifugal forces of language and tradition are even when a common currency leads to increased economic integration. Particular communities and even nations continue to resist homogenization into a single encompassing order. Yet, paradoxically, there is also a sense of pan-European identity. This larger sense of commonality testifies to the potential of a significantly inclusive community that is at the same time self-critical. While the criticism may be directed at the larger union in general or at other individual members, it also represents a comparative awareness that any particular perspective is partial and therefore limited.

The challenge is to avoid conceiving and institutionalizing the larger union in ways that gratuitously undermine and even denigrate more particular traditions. Meeting this challenge is admittedly daunting in view of the fact that a single currency is almost certain to be retained, and the almost inevitable correlative development is movement toward more commonality in fiscal policy and financial regulation and even more integration in labor markets. Daunting though it may be, it is not only feasible but also crucial to value the particular traditions of local and regional communities even as the larger union is embraced.

It is tempting to dismiss this valuing of particular traditions as little more than a nostalgic yearning for an irretrievable past. An analogue in the United States would be to mourn the attenuation of regional accents in an age of national electronic media. But even if local particularity almost unavoidably becomes less pronounced, it need not be denigrated. Indeed, to affirm and seek to preserve what is of value in local traditions can contribute to a more wholehearted embrace of the larger community. As this formulation suggests, any larger affirmation is inherently a critical and self-critical process, since it is not self-evident what is worth preserving in local traditions. But this process of assessment is emphatically preferable to a simple presumption that some least common denominator is the best or the only way forward.

## The Limits of Unlimited Secularism

Opposing this acknowledgement of limited and partial capacity are assertions of total control. Remarkably, the most potent instances of such assertions are secular adaptations—one is tempted to say heresies—of Jewish and Christian thought in the form of Marxism. As exemplified in both the Union of Soviet Socialist Republics (USSR) and the People's Republic of China (PRC), a version of totalitarian secular ideology attempts to preempt any and all allegiances to less inclusive communities.

The recent history of both the Soviet Union and Communist China demonstrates that this kind of totalitarian claim is difficult to sustain over the long term. As the Soviet Union dissolved, ethnic and linguistic segments of the USSR became differentiated countries, albeit with major interdependence between the new republics and especially with Russia. Even within Russia there remain massive tensions, in particular in areas that are predominantly Muslim. There are similar persistent tensions between the dominant Mandarin-speaking Han and multiple other discrete ethnic, linguistic, and even religious communities in the PRC.

In contemporary China and Russia, a resurgence of civil society adds to tensions. In China, for example, there is the emergence of a labor rights movement. Moreover, in both countries suppressed religious impulses are also reemerging. The challenge for such societies is to move from an all-encompassing secular order dominated by a single ethnic and linguistic group to arrangements that allow space for diverse groups and traditions that cannot indefinitely be suppressed.

This challenge is of course not confined to Russia and China. To take only two other instances, consider Turkey and France. France is perhaps the most insistent of any European country that it is a secular state, to the point that it often seems unaware of the cultural asymmetries that result from its history as part of Western Christendom. It therefore misses the irony, not to say perversity, of attempting to ban the wearing of Muslim headscarves while allowing crucifixes in public school classrooms. Here too a greater sense of inclusiveness together with a capacity for self-awareness and self-criticism would be welcome.

Like the Soviet Union, the PRC, and the French Republic, the Turkey of Mustafa Kemal Ataturk declared itself a resolutely secular state. The Ottoman Caliphate was officially abolished in 1924; Islamic courts were closed in 1926 and replaced with a civil code modeled on Swiss judicial processes. A unified educational system was established, designed to include girls as well as boys. And yet over several generations, subcommunities like the Kurds have resisted assimilation, and observant Muslims have over time reasserted the bearing on public policy of their religiously inspired traditions. In short, Turkey too is struggling toward a sense of community that is inclusive without simply suppressing particular traditions in favor of an allegedly neutral secular unity. In this respect, Turkey is further down the path that Egypt and Tunisia—from admittedly less resolutely secular starting points—will also have to tread. In all these cases, as well as others across the Middle East, the imperative is to affirm a sense of inclusive community that embraces multiple traditions and that allows the values of individualism with the overall order that a nontotalitarian state affords.

## Intercommunal Conflict Without an Established Secular Order

The current conflict in the Middle East illustrates the enormous challenge faced when an authoritarian system is widely repudiated without any settled arrangements for intercommunal relations.

In the case of Iraq after the fall of Saddam Hussein, a constitution was in fact written and approved. But the majority Shiite population—or at least its leaders—could not resist the temptation to seize control of virtually all government posts and ministries. Feeling aggrieved and very publicly expressing outrage, the Sunni population launched ferocious sectarian onslaughts, which of course elicited a violent government response. At the same time, the Kurds increasingly withdrew into Iraqi Kurdistan, focused on developing their own economic power and political institutions.

The case of Iraq demonstrates that achieving a society inclusive of diverse communities is not simply a matter of codifying constitutional arrangements. Instead, there must be a sustained cultivation of intercommunal relations that allows the building of long-term trust. The arrangements can be quite *ad hoc*, as was the case for decades in Lebanon. But there must be confidence that all parties will be allowed to participate and that power and its benefits will at least to a limited degree be shared.

The tragedy of Syria is that there is no such confidence. Under the Assad regime, a single community (the Alawites) within the Shia minority exercised strict control over political, military, and societal life even while allowing limited participation by other Shia and some members of Sunni communities. The authorities also provided some protection for the Kurdish minority as well as for the much smaller Christian and still smaller Jewish populations.

With the collapse of governing authority in much of the country, the wanton slaughter of over 200,000 citizens and the destruction of entire towns and cities constitute a catastrophe of enormous proportions. With over one-third of its population displaced from their homes and over three million more living as refugees in neighboring countries, Syria is hemorrhaging to such a degree that it will require decades to recover, all the more so with the additional variable of the Islamic State now stretching across the Iraq–Syria border and threatening further destabilization of the entire region.

Yet even in Syria, as I have argued in previous chapters, the only long-term way out is to reestablish an order that provides protection to all citizens and allows at least limited sharing of the benefits that participation in public life affords. Stating this condition cannot but seem to be pointing out the obvious or affirming a platitude. It is, however, crucial that this simple truism be embraced, since lasting peace and a semblance of security are attainable only if there is at least tolerance for and grudging acceptance of the requirement that disparate communities live together in more inclusive settings that allow and in some measure even respect the allegiances to which the more particular communities are committed.

## Conflict and Community in the Developing World

The world is regrettably replete with settings like Iraq and Syria where there is insufficient governmental authority to assure basic security for communities. Often referred to as "fragile states" or even "failed states," such settings pose their own challenges to the viability of inclusive communities. Yet in these instances as well, the most promising way forward is to build on the particular traditions that command respect rather than to attempt to suppress those traditions in favor of a comprehensive, externally imposed set of arrangements. Variations on this theme are endless; in Africa alone, dozens of examples suggest themselves. To represent a broad spectrum in terms of history and geography, I will refer again to two illuminatingly different cases, the Democratic Republic of the Congo and Afghanistan.

The Democratic Republic of Congo (DRC) suffers from massive disadvantages in terms of governance. It is a very large country (roughly the size of the entirety of Western Europe) with arbitrary borders determined by colonial powers; over two hundred language groups; and a history of egregiously bad rulers, from King Leopold II of Belgium (who acquired property rights to the Congo in 1885) through the corrupt and authoritarian regime of Mobutu Sese Seko (1971–1997). The DRC also has both the blessing and the curse of substantial natural resources. Its most critical challenge is to forge a process of governance that establishes and maintains a minimum of security and a sense of decentralized national identity while incorporating its remarkable ethnic and linguistic diversity.

Security, governance, and national identity are also critical to the prospects for Afghanistan. For over two millennia, Afghanistan has struggled with numerous invading forces; to name only three famous ones: the armies of Alexander the Great, Genghis Khan, and the Soviet Union. It has had to contend with fractious relations among its linguistically and ethnically diverse regions. Also on the horizon have been its powerful neighbors, eager to pursue their own interests and concerns. One salient lesson from this complex and contentious history is that Afghanistan does not long tolerate, or even allow, occupation by non-Afghan forces or government control from a central authority. Put positively, in order to have some chance of success, proposals for the governance of Afghanistan must incorporate particular traditions grounded in powerful local communities and from there build coalitions, almost certainly including at least tacit alliances with neighboring countries, that may in turn support a limited central government. Any effective sense of national identity must embrace the ethnic, linguistic, and religious pluralism that this process of consultation, negotiation, and collaboration implies.

## Toward a New Communitarianism

The tradition of voluntary associations, the struggles of the European Community, the resistance to government control of all of public life in thoroughly secular states, the tragedies of Iraq and Syria, and the conflicts in developing countries—all are variations on the same theme of how particular communities relate to more inclusive ones. The previous examples express in multiple ways that not only individuals in relation to the larger society but also traditional communities are crucial. Put more bluntly, claims that either individuals or the state can be abstracted from the traditions that shape them cannot be sustained. As a result, not only does totalitarianism collapse as a defensible ideology, but unqualified individualism is also not a viable position.

While this set of issues is certainly not new, it takes special salience today as traditional communities worldwide foster opposition to the individualism and secularism of the West. Under such circumstances, affirming the value of particular communities is the right course of action on both principled and pragmatic grounds. In acknowledging the historical particularity of its own traditions, the West opens up the prospect of participating in a community that is more inclusive in that it allows for both contributions and critical perspectives from multiple traditions.

The aim of such encounters among traditions should be a more self-critical and inclusive community that moves beyond state totalitarianism and unqualified individualism as well as the stances of uncritical and exclusionist traditionalists. Put positively, such interactions point toward a new communitarianism that affirms interactions among communities in search of such common ground as may be found. The intention of this process may be framed as achieving a more self-critical and inclusive community, even a world community. But grand statements of ultimate goals should not allow the quest for a prospective universal community to undermine actual particular communities. Instead, this aspiration for inclusive and self-critical communities must reach out from and build upon the particular traditions that animate existing local communities—including those that themselves are in fact or in intention also already part of existing global institutions, as in the world's three major missionary religions, Buddhism, Christianity, and Islam.

There is no shortage of international relations challenges for which this aspiration is directly relevant. The examples adduced here are a good start: the Democratic Republic of Congo, Afghanistan, Syria, Iraq, Turkey, the nations of former Soviet Union, China, the European Community, and the United States (not only in foreign affairs but also in domestic political interactions). All of these challenges cry out for a new communitarianism, one that affirms the contributions of particular traditions while also embracing the values of individualism as consistent with this sense of an inclusive and self-critical community.

# Conclusion

A NEW COMMUNITARIANISM is admittedly an abstract way of characterizing the challenge of moving beyond individualism to inclusive communities. For my part, I cannot but see direct relationships between my immersion in the texts of philosophers like Kant and Hegel (and also Plato, Augustine, Calvin, Spinoza, and many others) on the one hand and, on the other, the tensions between the individual and his or her communities—and therefore between individualism and communitarianism. I also feel a visceral connection between what I know are abstractions to almost everyone and the concrete experiences and actions in conflict situations.

In this book, I have tried to relate my own sense of such connections through an examination of central themes in education and action over more than a decade. The result is a hybrid of a memoir and a series of systematic reflections on core issues that confront all of us who seek to be responsible both as individuals and as faithful members of the communities to which we are committed. My hope is that readers will be intrigued at the prospect of exploring this double responsibility for themselves.

To affirm the community as well as the individual entails (even for the committed secularist) embracing the particular in terms of symbolic ideas and ritualized practices. At the same time, to value both the individual and the community allows—and may even require—openness to the universal. "Inclusive communities" is the deliberately restrained way that I have framed this openness to and advancement toward universality. Universal inclusion is almost certainly utopian in the sense Sir Thomas More intended when he coined the term from "u-topie," literally (in Greek) "no place." Yet the thrust toward universality is still valuable because it focuses attention on the need to seek ever greater inclusion.

Seeking ever greater inclusion may seem like little more than the utopian aspiration of a head-in-the-clouds idealist. I plead guilty to being an idealist in both the philosophical sense (I find Hegel more persuasive than his detractors, to take what is for me a salient example) and also in the more down-to-earth meaning of not easily settling for so-called "realistic" solutions to pressing problems. But seeking greater inclusion cannot only be an aspiration that idealists cherish. It is also an imperative if the international community is going to have any prospect of addressing the crisis of sustained conflict among communities that share a common location. For that reason, the quest for greater inclusion is a worthy ideal and also a practical requirement.

To help all of us to recognize and act on this practical requirement is the core intention of this book. Greater inclusion certainly does not require homogeneity. Indeed, its defining characteristic is its capacity to incorporate even widely divergent views, which in principle can include both the religiously committed and convinced secularists. While I have not always been aware of it, this goal has been at the heart of my activities for the past five decades. In a sense this book is just one more appeal to enlist others in what I deem to be a crucial global quest for increasingly inclusive communities.

# Index

CERC. *See* Center for Environmental Research and Conservation

Ceylon. *See* Sri Lanka

China: and declining viability of totalitarianism, 167–68; importance of studying culture of, 31; inability to fully suppress traditional culture and religion, 175; and inclusive communities, necessity of creating, 180; international students in, 71; peaceful coexistence of religions in, 15, 22

Christian conservatives in U.S., outsider views on, 155–56

Christianity: Buddhist beliefs about, 35; communal basis of identity in, 77–78, 170; as dominant European tradition, 22; human relation to nature in, and ecological threat, 157–59, 164–65; human responsibility to Earth's ecosystem in, 157–59; idea of humans as part of whole in, 164–65; individual as constituted through community in, 20; missionary impulse of, and engagement with non-Western traditions, 44; role in creation of inclusive, self-critical communities, 180; truth claims of, diversity of beliefs and, 14

Christian Right, growing influence of, 12

Church Peace Union, 144–46

civilian casualties, contemporary rise of internecine conflicts and, 104–5

civil liberties, respect for in inclusive communities, 79

civil rights movement: author's involvement with, 1, 2, 3; and slow pace of change, 2

clichés, characterization of truths as, as means of avoiding action, 98

Cold War, 104

colleges and universities, Japanese, challenges facing, 53–54; declining public funding as, 57, 59; excess institutional capacity as, 54–55, 70–73; as less pressing for elite institutions, 54–55; recruitment of international students and, 71–73; strategies for addressing, 70–73

colleges and universities, Japanese, high number of private institutions, 58

colleges and universities, U.S.: and ecological threat, inquiry into, 160–63; enrollment in private *vs.* public institutions, 57–58; as exemplifications of individualism, 160–61; need for multidisciplinary study in, 161; private, high number of, 57, 58; public institutions, rising tuition and fees at, 58; values learned in, 80, 89. *See also* education

colleges and universities, U.S., and global perspective: courses on globalization, value of, 30–31; diversity of student body, benefits of, 33; foreign language study, importance of, 30, 31–32; and international curriculum,

colleges and universities, U.S., and global perspective (*continued*)
need for, 32; and minority perspectives, importance of including, 33; and preparation for inclusive communities, 53; and reversal of U.S. provincialism, 27, 28–30, 30–32, 38; study abroad, benefits of, 33, 34–38; study of foreign cultures and languages, decline in, 29, 31–32; study of foreign cultures and languages, difficulties of implementing, 32, 33

colleges and universities, U.S., challenges facing: availability of well-prepared students as, 53, 55–57, 67–70, 73; clear expression of institutional identity as solution to, 53, 59–69; declining public funding as, 53, 57–59, 68–70; *vs.* Japanese institutions, 53–54, 57, 59; as less pressing for elite institutions, 55; rising tuition and fees as, 58–59

colleges and universities, U.S., institutional identity of: at Columbia University, refinement of, 64–67; institutional history as necessary basis of, 59, 68; as key to addressing other challenges, 59–60; positive effects of clear expression of, 53, 59–69; at Rice University, refinement of, 60–63; shaping of future prospects by, 59

Columbia Earth Institute (Columbia University), 66, 161–63

Columbia University: author at, 5–6, 64–67; ecological and climate research at, 161–63; South Asian Institute, 129

Columbia University, refocusing of institutional identity of, 64–67; administrative changes and, 64; and enrollment of foreign students, 68; as example rather than model, 54; and excellence of undergraduate education as asset, 66–68; and global standing as asset, 66; and New York City location as asset, 64–66; relations with neighboring communities, 65–66; success of, 67–69

comic distance, and the good life, 81

commitment: to cause larger than self, and the good life, 81–84; as ongoing concern of author, 1

common good, disciplining of individual initiative to as 21st century challenge, 86

communities: as check on individual, in theories of individualism, 17–19; as circles of increasing inclusiveness surrounding individuals, 89–94; globalization as source of increasing emphasis on, 20–21; importance of for human flourishing, 111–14, 132; importance of including poor persons in, 88; necessity of valuing above individualism, 21; as ongoing concern of author, 1; of others, learning from, 95–96, 98; participation in as goal for good life, 93–94; undermining of by unrestrained capitalism and individualism, 20; well-ordered, importance of good government for, 111–14, 123. *See also* inclusive communities; religious communities; traditional communities

communities, and globalization: increasing emphasis on need for community, 20–21; multiple models for inclusive communities, 21–23; undermining of traditional communities as 21st century issue, 86, 87; unified global community as utopian dream, 87–88, 181–82

communities, local: as circle within increasingly inclusive communities, 89; linkages to other communities, 89–90; strengthening of as goal, 88. *See also* local capacity, building of

Community-Driven Reconstruction Program in Democratic Republic of the Congo, 131–32

comparative appraisal of beliefs: and acceleration of changes in belief, 51; by adherents of religious groups, 47; development of criteria for through comparative study of religions,

48–50, 51; dynamic between descriptive and normative adequacy and, 49–51; engagement with non-Western traditions and, 44–46, 47, 51–52; need for, 13–15

comparative study of religions: adherents' participation in, 47; cross-cultural understanding encouraged by, 44; and development of objective evaluative criteria, 48–49, 49–50; as Enlightenment innovation, 43; at Harvard, 40–41; ongoing value of, modern resurgence of religious faith and, 46–48; productivity of, 43–44; as source of cosmopolitanism, 39; undermining of traditional religious authority by, 14–15, 48–49

comparative study of religions, separation of from theology: collapse of in comparative interrogation of one's own values, 44–45; Harvard's collapsing of, 41, 42; as recent historical development, 43; as typical, 42–44

conflict within and between religions, long tradition of, 47

Confucianism: coexistence with other Asian religions, 15, 22; communal basis of identity in, 77, 170; individual as constituted through community in, 19

conservatives, increasing visibility of, 12

consumer society: and removal of
individual from community, 78–79,
171; as social system without ethical
grounding, 23

conviction: definition of, 12–13; in a
pluralistic world, 11–13

convictions, strongly-held: examples of,
12; globalization's undermining of
truth claims of, 14–15; as inviable position, 11–12, 13; as typically limited
to small communities, 12; Yeats on,
12–13

cotton, African, and unfair global competition, 115

Council for Ethics in International Affairs, 145

Council on Ethics and International
Affairs, 145

Council on Religion and International
Affairs, 145

critical thinking: and the good life, 80; as
product of liberal education, 80

cross-cultural study, necessity of examining one's own values in, 46

culture of inclusion, welcoming of immigrants and, 127–29

cynicism, as risk of liberal education, 80

Darfur refugees, IRC programs for,
110–11

Dead Sea, as metaphor for self-involvement, 82–83, 84

death, Western attitude toward, as 21st

century challenge, 86–87

Democratic Republic of the Congo
(DRC): history of, 111–12; and
inclusive community, necessity
of creating, 178, 180; IRC health
surveys in, 112–13; IRC programs in,
131–32; village-based development
councils in, 131–32

Democratic Republic of the Congo
(DRC), conflict in, 112; deaths attributed to, 112–13; and need for sound
government, 113–14

dependency of developing nations, foreign aid and, 96–97, 98, 109–11, 123

descriptive adequacy of religious
beliefs: as criterion in comparative
evaluation of religions, 49–51; issues
requiring resolution through, 50

developed world: aid from, and charges
of neocolonialism, 155; difficulty
of absorbing immigrants, 122;
increasing recognition of need for
open borders in, 121–22; and models
for religion as resource in conflict
resolution, 155–56; necessity of
increasing aid from, 115–18

developing world: impact of adequate
aid on, 118; wealth gap with
developed world, as 21st century
challenge, 86

development agencies: BRAC's success
as, 139–41; education programs, opportunities for collaboration on, 142;

Francis of Assisi, Saint, 158
free-market economics. See *laissez-faire*
    capitalism
Future Generations Graduate School, 142

Garang, John, 8
gender roles, traditional, undermining of
    by Western individualism, 76
General Agreement on Tariffs and
    Trade (GATT), Uruguay Round,
    developed nations' poor compliance
    with, 114–15
Germany: author's studies in, 2–3, 4,
    34–35; and immigration, 122; inter-
    national students in, 71; resistance to
    absorbing immigrants, 122
Global 30 Project for Establishing Core
    Universities for Internationalization,
    72–73
globalization: complex process included
    within, 120–21; courses to increase
    awareness of, 30–32; and danger of
    viewing world through U.S.-dom-
    inated perspective, 30, 31; ensuring
    benefits of for poor nations, 114–15,
    116; exacerbation of individualism
    by, 87; and increasing migration
    of people, 121; increasing pace and
    scope of, 121; and knowledge of
    other cultures, importance of, 30–31;
    and *laissez-faire* capitalism, 20;
    nurturing of both local communi-
    ties and global connections in, 76,
    169; as overall positive force, 86;

undermining of claims of religious
    authority by, 14–15
globalization and community: increas-
    ing emphasis on, 20–21; multiple
    models for inclusive communities,
    21–23; undermining of traditional
    communities as 21st century issue,
    86, 87; unified global community as
    utopian dream, 87–88, 181–82
God's relation to nature, and ecological
    threat, 158–59, 164–65
good life: aiming high and, 79–80;
    American conception of from indi-
    vidual perspective, 74–75; balancing
    of values of individualism with
    inclusive community in, 79; com-
    mitment to cause larger than self
    and, 81–84; "letting go" and, 80–81;
    participation in communities and,
    93–94; purely individual focus as
    inadequate for, 74–75
government: importance of for well-
    ordered communities, 111–14, 123;
    necessity of valuing above markets,
    20–21; U.S. tradition of criticizing, 114

Harvard Divinity School: author at, 3–4,
    5–6, 41; establishment of, 40; links to
    Arts and Sciences faculty, 41, 42
Harvard University, establishment of, 39
Harvard University, history of religious
    studies at, 39–42; Committee on the
    Study of Religion, 41, 42–43; histori-
    cal/comparative study, 40–41;

normative adequacy and, 49–51; engagement with non-Western traditions and, 44–46, 47, 51–52; need for, 13–15; as opportunity for self-criticism, 16

religious bodies with premium on decision to join as example of voluntary associations, 173

religious communities: extremes of provincialism of, 39; potential for change in, 164; power of, blindness of secular individualism to, 9

religious extremism, recent resurgence of, and ongoing value of religious studies, 46–48

religious institutions, role in action on ecological threat, 163–66

religious persons: ongoing comparative appraisal of beliefs by, 47; unwillingness to separate faith from public life, 15–16

religious studies: contributions to study of the humanities, 44–46, 47, 51–52; at Harvard University, history of, 39–41; as model of responsible approach to normative questions, 45–46, 52; ongoing value of, 46–48, 52. *See also* comparative study of religions; theological study

religious tolerance, history of, 103–4

Rice Quantum Institute, 62–63

Rice Student Volunteer Program (RSVP), 90

Rice University: author at, 5–6, 60–63, 90; community outreach programs at, 90

Rice University, refocusing institutional identity of, 60–63; administrative changes in, 61–62; and creation of multidisciplinary centers, 62–63; curriculum changes and, 63; and distinctive features, emphasis of, 60–61; as example rather than model, 54; success of, 68

Ritsumeikan Asia-Pacific University, 72

Roberts, Les, 112

Rupp, George: addresses to students by, 85; background and education, 1–8, 119–20, 127; at Columbia University, 5–6, 64–67; commitment to new communitarianism, 182; experiences with study abroad, 34–36; experience with U.S. immigration, 119–20; at Harvard Divinity School, 3–4, 5–6, 41; involvement in Vietnam War protests, 1, 3; involvement with civil rights movement, 1, 2, 3; involvement with International Rescue Committee (IRC), 5, 6–9, 92, 135–36; at Johnston College, University of Redlands, 3; multicultural extended family of, 127–28; residence in Sri Lanka (Ceylon), 1–2, 3, 35; at Rice University, 5–6, 60–63, 90; in South Sudan, 7–8; studies in Germany, 2–3, 4, 34–35; study of

Rupp, George (*continued*)
    Buddhism, 2, 3, 35, 147; travels in
    Africa, 5, 6, 92; travels in Asia, 3, 5,
    6, 92, 125; travels in Europe, 2, 3; at
    University of Wisconsin-Green Bay,
    4–5; visits to Afghanistan, 6–7, 92
Rupp, Kathy (daughter), 1–2, 5, 35, 71
Rupp, Nancy (wife), xii, 1–2, 4, 5, 35, 94,
    127–28
Rupp, Stephanie (daughter), 2–3, 5, 94
Russia: and declining viability of
    totalitarianism, 168; ethnic tensions
    in, 175
Rwanda: DRC conflict and, 111–12; IRC
    programs in, 131

sacred texts, globalization's undermining
    of truth claims of, 14
Salt Lake City, welcoming of immigrants
    by, 37, 38
Saudi Arabia, and declining viability of
    totalitarianism, 167–68
Save the Children: emphasis on building
    local capacity, 143; organizational
    structure of, 136, 138
Sea of Galilee, as metaphor for openness
    to others, 82–83, 84
secular individualism: alternatives to
    as model for inclusive communi-
    ties, 21–23; blindness to power of
    religious communities, 9; broad op-
    position to among religious persons,
    16; necessity of change in, as area of

agreement for external and internal
    critics, 23. *See also* individualism,
    Western
secularism, unlimited, inability to
    suppress traditional culture and
    religion, 175–76
secular liberalism: as appropriation of
    Western religion, 165; as dominant
    global view, 12; perceived unwilling-
    ness to engage religious traditions
    on equal terms, 51–52; self-criticism
    of, comparative study of beliefs as
    avenue toward, 52
secular liberalism, on religion as private,
    12; as unacceptable to religious
    persons, 15–16; as untenable posi-
    tion, 13–14
self-criticism: diversity of beliefs within
    religions as opportunity for, 16; in
    inclusive communities, 79, 171; in
    secular liberalism, comparative
    study of beliefs as avenue toward,
    52; by United States, other nations'
    complaints as means toward, 89.
    *See also* inclusive, self-critical com-
    munities
self-involvement, escape from, as source
    of renewed life, 81–84
self-righteous moralism of U.S., other
    nations' complaints about, 89
self-understanding, study abroad and,
    34–35, 36
sense of humor, and the good life, 81

turnover of programs to local employees,
benefits of, 109, 130, 135–36, 141
21st century challenges, 85–87; necessity
of confronting as community, 87;
uncritical individualism as root
of, 87
*Two Treatises of Civil Government*
(Locke), 17

Uganda: and declining viability of totalitarianism, 168; DRC conflict and, 112
unilateral action by U.S.: collapse of Soviet Union and, 104; other nations'
complaints about, 89
unionization, and deprofessionalization
of teachers, 56
United Kingdom: BRAC and, 140;
foreign aid by, 117–18; and immigration, 122; international students in,
71; tradition of voluntary associations, and possibility of inclusive,
self-critical communities, 172–73
United Nations: Church Peace Union as
advocate of, 145; and Darfur crisis,
110; peacekeeping forces of, 115; and
postwar peace activism, 150–51
United States: campaign financing
as issue in, 156; decline of global
standing, 28, 88; and foreign aid,
inadequate contributions to, 92–93,
116–18; generosity of, mistaken
public opinion on, 92, 116–17; glar-
ing deficiencies in political process

of, 156; illusion of self-subsistence
in, 91; and inclusive communities,
necessity of creating, 180; intercon-
nection with other nations, 91; international students in, 71; as model
of religious tolerance, 155–56; new
appreciation of, study abroad and,
34–35; other nations' complaints
about, 71–72; past monoculture
of as myth, 122; self-criticism by,
other nations' complaints as means
toward, 89; separation of church and
state in, 104, 156; stalled legislative
process as issue in, 156; uncritical
assumptions in foreign policy of, 28.
*See also* colleges and universities,
U.S.; provincialism, American
United States and illegal immigration:
necessity of citizenship for illegal
immigrants, 127; and need to address issues in sending countries,
122; as policy issue, 122; relationships
with home nation and, 127
United States and immigration:
antiterrorism legislation and,
124–25; author's experience with,
119–20; contributions of immigrants,
126–27; culture of inclusion and,
127–29; immigrant remittances to
home nations, 126–27; melting pot
*vs.* salad/mosaic metaphors for, 127,
128–29; needed reforms in immigration policies and procedures,

United States and immigration (*cont.*)
124–26; need for larger number of
immigrants, 124, 125–26; and new-
comer ties to place of origin, valuing
of, 126–27, 127–29; recent decline in
admission of migrants, 121; relatively
open U.S. labor market, 121; resettlement of refugees in, 37, 106–7, 131;
stresses of multiple cultural traditions, 122; tradition of welcoming
immigrants, 119–20, 121, 122; U.S. as
nation of immigrants and, 121, 122,
129; U.S.'s relative acceptance of immigrants, 122, 129
universities. *See entries under* colleges
and universities
University of Wisconsin-Green Bay,
author at, 4–5
Uruguay Round, developed nations'
poor compliance with, 114–15

values of one's own: failure to interro-
gate, as analogous to close-minded
religious faith, 45; interrogation of
through engagement with other religious traditions, 44–46, 47, 179–80;
necessity of evaluating, 13–15; recognizing historical particularity of as
key to inclusiveness, 179–80
Vietnam War: author's involvement in
protests against, 1, 3; and changing
face of war, 104, 146

viewpoint, single, inadequacy of, 3, 13
village-based development councils,
131–32
voluntary associations, and possibility of
inclusive, self-critical communities,
172–73

warfare: contemporary rise of internecine conflicts, 104–5; history of,
103–4, 146; traditional conventions
of, 104, 146
wealth gap: as consequence of unrestrained capitalism and individualism, 20; and economic development programs, need for, 97; and
education opportunities, 58–59, 70;
increase of, and urgency of reform,
9; necessity of closing, 21, 130; as 21st
century challenge, 86; between U.S.
and Cameroon, 96–97
wealthy persons: isolation of from community, 90; as only beneficiaries of
tax cuts, 21
Western hedonism and materialism:
consumer society as product of, 23;
necessity of critical evaluation of,
16–17; traditional societies' complaints about, 16, 88–89
Western individualism. *See* individualism, Western
Western secularism. *See entries under*
secularism

White, Lynn, 157–59, 164

Wilson, Woodrow, 27–28

women and girls: benefits of empowering, 142; importance of education for, 92; IRC education of in Afghanistan, 108; Muslim resistance to programs for, 108, 153–54

women's liberation, and deprofessionalization of teachers, 56

World Bank, 108, 132–33, 134

World Conference of Religion for Peace, 151

World Food Summit (1996), 115–16

World Vision International: emphasis on building local capacity, 143; organizational structure of, 136–37;

and religion as resource for conflict resolution, 154

World War I, peace activism following, 150

World War II: IRC work in, 106; peace activism following, 150

world-wide networks, as circle within increasingly inclusive communities, 91

Wright, John, 151

Yale University, separation of divinity and religious studies at, 42

Yeats, William Butler, 12–13

Zimbabwe, and declining viability of totalitarianism, 167, 168

*Religion, Culture, and Public Life*
SERIES EDITOR: KAREN BARKEY

*After Pluralism: Reimagining Religious Engagement*, edited by Courtney Bender and Pamela E. Klassen

*Religion and International Relations Theory*, edited by Jack Snyder

*Religion in America: A Political History*, Denis Lacorne
*Democracy, Islam, and Secularism in Turkey*, edited by Ahmet T. Kuru and Alfred Stepan

*Refiguring the Spiritual: Beuys, Barney, Turrell, Goldsworthy*, Mark C. Taylor

*Tolerance, Democracy, and Sufis in Senegal*, edited by Mamadou Diouf

*Rewiring the Real: In Conversation with William Gaddis, Richard Powers, Mark Danielewski, and Don DeLillo*, Mark C. Taylor

*Democracy and Islam in Indonesia*, edited by Mirjam Künkler and Alfred Stepan

*Religion, the Secular, and the Politics of Sexual Difference*, edited by Linell E. Cady and Tracy Fessenden

*Recovering Place: Reflections on Stone Hill*, Mark C. Taylor

*Boundaries of Toleration*, edited by Alfred Stepan and Charles Taylor

*Choreographies of Sharing at Sacred Sites: Religion, Politics, and Conflict Resolution*, edited by Elazar Barkan and Karen Barkey